To the innocent victims of terrorism around the globe; my parents for being noble humanitarians; my wife for her integrity and dedication; my daughters for their untiring love; my students for creating critical thinking in me; and for all the future generations of mankind with a genuine wish that they find the ways to live in a nonviolent world through the 21st century and beyond

Preface

My Interest in the Study of Violence

Realizing that many people of my generation were exposed to atrocities during World War II, my personal perplexity about violence started at an early age; it was at the time of the partition of India and Pakistan in 1947. I was about five years of age then. Since my father was a ranking officer in the State Government in India, we resided in a large government house in a corner of an old fort located in the northwestern town, not far from the newly created border of the two nations. Next, to the west of my house lived a lawyer's family. Our roofs were adjoining so I often crossed over to that family's house to play off and on with a little girl named Razi and her younger brother. Razi was of my own age. We enjoyed talking about our families, including how we both had different religions. However, in our childish chats we perhaps did not realize the seriousness of the differences in our family faiths until the time of the partition when India was arbitrarily divided into two nations by the British Government. People of the two major religions in India were assigned the territories in three different regions of the country. Millions of people 'belonging' to two different faiths/religions were forced out of their homes and communities abandoning their ancestral properties and moved to their respective regions, causing a chaos and anarchy perhaps never experienced anywhere in the world before. In a state of lawlessness and confusion, watched helplessly by the militaries and police authorities, riots broke out in various parts of India, leading to lootings and killings based only on 'known' religious affiliations of people involved. I remember the most horrible night during that period when I heard a lot of noise of lootings and fire shots on the side of Razi's house. I could not sleep the whole night worrying about the safety of my friends. At the sunrise, I quietly crossed over the roof to her house despite strict instructions from my parents and I saw the mutilated bodies of Razi's family. I saw Razi lying on the floor with a pool of blood around her head. I came back crying and developed high fever for several days. My parents were told by someone that I probably was possessed by Razi's ghost. Even today, I remember her innocent face looking terrified as she lay dead. I still have no clue as to why anyone could mercilessly kill a beautiful little girl and her innocent little brother!

In addition to the above incident, I witnessed a horrifying scene involving a young girl being brutally molested by a crowd of men in a marketplace during the time of partition. They ignored very young boys watching the horrifying act. I also observed a large number of the so-called refugees—people who had been forced to move from their homes in each country involved. I used to watch with awe the cases of destitute people begging public officials for help. I even witnessed a train full of passengers parked at our railway station with hundreds of dead bodies of men, women and children. I asked my elders why violence based on religion was happening, but did not get much response to satisfy my curiosity. I felt that tall and solid social walls had been built around human beings based on religion or creed. For sure, I became interested from my very young age in the phenomenon of violence in which human beings engaged against each other in various forms. I often wondered how phenomena related to violence are the realities of human lives just like love, compassion and tenderness are! I started to ponder over various forms and means of interpersonal violence people are engaged in and appear to, and even justify what they do in that regard. However, I started becoming optimistic about the future of mankind after reading (during my college days in the late 1950s and early 1960s) the works of Mahatma Gandhi, Jawaharlal Nehru, Rabindranath Tagore, Bertrand Russell, Leo Tolstoy, and Swami Vivekananda. All of them had a liberal and constructive outlook towards human sense of justice and prospects of secularism in the world. I felt that they and other philosophers I read in those years expressed a lot of optimism for an increasing progress towards, social equality and peace in our lives.

I later became intellectually involved in the topic of violence in my teaching during the mid 1970s when I started teaching in the U.S. For example, when I was preparing to teach a course on family violence from a sociological perspective, I became overwhelmed by various media reports, though sketchy and folksy, talking particularly about child as well as spousal abuses in the country. I had also become cognizant of child neglect and wife abuse in the patriarchal societies in various other parts of the globe where probably, taboos or denials existed in talking about such dark sides of family life. However, I could find no book that dealt with family violence in scientific and comprehensive ways. I do want to report though that there has been a significant increase in systematic scientific studies and availability of books on various forms and dimensions of family violence, during the past three decades. Even media and entertainment industry has gotten involved in publicizing preventive strategies for violence against children, women, elderly, and lower castes. I myself became involved in scholarly research on subjects such as 'bride burning' incidents in India, 'honor killing' in particular sub-cultures, and sexual abuse of children in America.

Then we were overwhelmed by the 9/11 incidents in New York City and Washington, D.C. I started teaching courses on suicide terrorism as well as on terrorism in general after the incidents because I believe that teaching is the best way of learning on the subject. I have been publishing as well as presenting papers on the subject based on my research during the past several years. I decided to develop a manuscript on terrorism in 2003 and went through various phases of writing the book you are looking at. As you will read, this book expresses some of my disappointments about an increasing trend towards an enhanced scope of various forms of violence, some are unique to the 21st century (for example, suicide terrorism, cyber attacks, expansion of prospects for the use of weapons of mass destruction, complexity of crimes against the humanity based on the technological innovation, and so forth).

Focus in the Book on Terrorism as a Form of Violence

Although some of the ideas stated in the book may be relevant or applicable to multiple forms and styles of violence (discussed in chapter 2), my major focus is centered only on terrorism (discussed in chapter 3 and implied in other chapters), which is conceived to be a somewhat unique form of human violence.

No Mention of Historical, Political or Religions Events

After teaching on terrorism courses in sociology and criminology during the past ten years, I have realized that most of the research papers and books on the subject had focused on religious or political groups, and specific historical incidents or events of particular nations, and names of characters involved in such incidents. In this book, I have not gone over any micro-level data, stating names of countries, political groups, individuals, or religions that occur in my discussions. However, I have referred to selected information on specific authors and names of studies under various numbered endnotes on each chapter given towards the end of the book for those readers who are interested in additional information on various topics of terrorism. I believe that name calling in terms of political, national, and religious affiliations does not necessarily help critical thinking. Instead, we need to objectively and conceptually examine our problems or issues related to serious forms of violence at hand and reflect on selected topics. Thus, I have done my best to keep an impartial and objective outlook by completely avoiding any discussions in any emotionally charged manner or sensationalism. I have focused only on types or forms, general impacts, explanations, and preventive measures of violence, without appeasing or insulting particular vested interests, if any. I believe that by concentrating on conceptual analysis of the terrorist phenomena, I have enabled readers to look at a 'bigger picture', examining the issues involved, instead of resorting to incidental enumerations or name calling.

No Easy Answers Either

There is no easy understanding of a complex situation of terrorism; no easy answers to many questions puzzling us about the issue over the years; no oversimplification of conclusions we may arrive at; and no hasty decisions on the so-called solutions. Although I have tried to address the problems related to terrorism and attempted to talk about various options for prevention, I was cautious in stating closures or 'final' words on the subject as such. Similarly, although I have interest in the sociological perspective on violence, I have chosen to be simple and straightforward without using much of technical jargon and authors' names in the text of this book, so that I am comprehensible to academic readers in humanities, social and hard sciences, as well as to general readers.

A Book with a Different Outlook and Style

In this book, I have made statements in a personalized, though logically and theoretically meaningful way. I wanted to focus on direct language aimed at trying to understand issues and concepts at a global level, relevant to terrorism as a problem with more focus on 'what' and 'why', without meddling with details where we get into subjective and popular media type concerns about 'who' and 'where'. However, I do not imply that my approach is better than ones used by other books on terrorism and violence. It is just different. For example, several books focusing on individual case studies and specific incidents of violence are highly respectable and make meaningful contributions in their own way.[1]

I have in this book, approached violence in both realistic and constructive ways. I often tell my students that we need to be preventive and optimistic in dealing with all sorts of nasty violence in human society. I have not pursued a doom and gloom approach in this book despite an increase in new forms of violence as I have mentioned above. As you will read, I have presented no popular formulas for 'solving' problems of violence and terrorism. I have been careful in making statements in the book without implying any over-simplifications or over-generalizations. I was straight and simple in summarizing various topics to provide the readers a glimpse of what the issues or human problems are, what some of their consequences are, and what selected possible preventive strategies could be (without implying any advocacy of any particular moral and political ideologies as such). I have not implied any favor towards (or 'preaching' on) whatever ideological notions (such as non-violence, democracy, and secularism) I have talked about.

Chapter Scheme

Chapter 1 introduces the reader to the outlook or approach of writing this book. It goes over the goal and justification of studying an overview of various forms of terrorism, and the use of critical thinking perspective as well as a constructive outlook used in approaching the topic. Chapter 1 also goes over the theoretical frame of reference and research methodology I have used, through partially funded research to study various topics in the book during the past several years. Chapters 2, 3 and 4 provide a conceptual background to study terrorism. Chapter 2 covers a discussion on the reality, styles and dimensions of violence in human society as a general background for terrorism. Chapter 3 provides an overview of the process and types of terrorism as a unique form of a sort of a 'dirty and atypical' warfare in human society. Chapter 4 focuses on a unique and significantly increasing form of violence called suicide terrorism (hereafter referred to in the book as 'terrorcide', a term I coined for a reason of brevity).

Chapter 5 deals with identifying explanation and impact of terrorism. Chapter 6 specifically addresses the use (and abuse) of the institution of religion by some individuals or groups, for rationalizing violence against the humanity. Finally, chapters 7 and 8 conclude the discussion on the subject by engaging in a constructive dialogue based on selected strategies for preventing terrorism into the future. Notions under the headings of secularism and non-violence are particularly aimed at rational as well as idealistically articulated preventive actions in these two chapters.

The book touches upon almost every aspect related to terrorism. It will be useful for policymakers, administrators, those concerned with maintaining law and order in society, security personnel, etc. It will also benefit the students, teachers and researchers in sociology, particularly terrorism. To those who wish to know about various issues related to terrorism and the measures to prevent and combat terrorism, it will provide for a richly rewarding reading.

R.N. Singh

Acknowledgements

I am thankful to my graduate and undergraduate students, who during the past many years, have become the prime source of inspiration for me. Many of them assisted in my research work and many inspired me to learn more to keep up with their untiring questions and interests in my teaching. I particularly recognize the work of Sudhir Agrawal, Sherry Boyer, Brandi Dial, Bill Elliott, Christina Gammon, Craig Maxwell, Bobby Moodley, Connie Taylor, and Doug Whitten.

I am indebted for encouragement and support from my mentors and colleagues, particularly Gurnam Saran Bhatnagar, K. Lawrence Clinton, Jerry S. Davis, Victor S. D'Souza, Harold F. Kaufman, Keith D. McFarland, Naresh Bandhu Roy, William E. Thompson, and Kenneth P. Wilkinson. Some of my colleagues who worked with me on research projects include Amir Abbassi, Vicki Davis, James R. McBroom, Mathew Kanjirathinkal, Steven S. Shwiff, Dharam Pal Singh, Jiaming Sun, and N. Prabha Unnithan. I am beholden to them.

I am grateful to the faculty at the Punjabi University for inviting me to participate in two major symposia at the university, one on "Violence: Impact and Intervention" in 2007, and the other on "Secularism and Violence: A Gateway to Peace" in 2009. Finally, I acknowledge the financial support in part from the Office of Graduate Studies and Research, Texas A&M University-Commerce, for enabling me to collect data on profiling suicide terrorists, identifying typologies and characteristics of violence as well as non-violence and exploring preventive strategies to tackle terrorism for developing and empirically validating multi-dimensional scales to measure secularism, assertiveness, and non-violence.

R.N. Singh

List of Tables

Contents

1

Overview of Contents and Approach

Man can only go forward by developing his reason, by finding a new harmony, a human one, instead of the pre-human harmony which is irretrievably lost.

—Erich Fromm

But the real conflicts are between bad, limited, or distorted religion and pure and high religion; and between limited and grudging science and science full and unafraid.

—Julian Huxley

The infinite meant, it was true, something forever untraversed even by thought, and hence something forever unknown—no matter how great [an] attainment in learning. But this 'forever unknown', instead of being chilling and repelling, was now an inspiring challenge to ever-renewed inquiry and an assurance of inexhaustible possibilities of progress.

—John Dewey

I plan to address in this book a timely topic involving a serious and unique form of violence called terrorism. It has been emerging rapidly in various forms during the past few decades in various parts of the globe. I will discuss selected aspects of terrorism through the critical and conceptual thinking perspective. I will be particularly outlining systematically its typologies, explanations, impacts, and preventive strategies in the following seven chapters of the book.

EXPECTED CONTRIBUTION OF THE BOOK

Presentations in the Book

Studies on violence and terrorism generally contribute to the literature used by those trying to reduce the economic and social costs associated with threats and occurrences of those phenomena. I expect that my book has some implications making an impact on our consciousness of this form of serious violence along with getting ideas toward a struggle for its future prevention. It seems that the United Nations' 2005 Summit on Peace Building neglected to establish the responsibility of all nations to prevent terrorism in the future.[1] I believe that we need to overcome pessimism with regard to the future of violence in the world and start making concerted efforts in developing our ability to predict and realize the potential for preventing and minimizing violent deaths of innocent people in the future. That position can only materialize if we affirm and continue to reaffirm professional (and personal) interests of sociologists, criminologists, psychologists, and investigators from multiple fields and perspectives to prevent deadly violence.[2] I hope my book has some implications for legislators, law enforcement agencies, and pro-active leaders by identifying ways of early detection and prevention of possible terrorist threats in the future. It may reflect on how and why terrorist individuals and groups become 'marginalized' and 'isolated' by societies at large in significant ways for their unreasonable use of violence against the humanity. Ideas based on my initial research may be useful for initiating additional studies in various parts of the world.

As I stated earlier in the Preface, I have attempted to take in this book a conceptual outlook than historical and other descriptions of terrorist events and particular names of political and religious groups involved in those incidents. Instead, I am focusing in my chapters only on concepts and selected typologies[3] based on empirical data and indulge in some critical discussions on relevant ideas and issues. I have used an analytical approach in outlining characteristics and categories of selected aspects of the terrorist phenomena. My conceptual typologies may be suggestive to developing theoretical and methodological sophistication in the field by diverting our attention from sensationalism, fear mongering, and name-calling descriptions of specific terrorist incidents (thereby identifying piece-meal and remedial strategies that are probably meant to provide us an occasional relief from violence now and then) to diagnostic and preventive (or curative) ideas for long-term planning instead.

Globalization Orientation

Several studies in the recent past have been conceptualizing understanding of terrorism from a global perspective.[4] We already see an increasing trend in the literature on terrorism recognizing comparative and broader applications of concepts and international data. Researchers are now more than ever developing new ideas interpreting rising trends of global linkages, cross-cultural-interconnectivities, and cross-cultural interdependences, including power sharing and developing alliances for combating common problems shared by multiple nations. Progressive and constructive outlooks are growing in our 'post-modern' age with increasing opportunities for diversity and open communication.[5] It seems to me that our younger generations do not seem to have much interest to going back to tribal and racist world. They are probably moving ahead with more and more interest in becoming 'international citizens' with an excitement for newer technology, cosmopolitanism, mobility, and liberal outlooks for relationships and interactions. Terrorism does not seem to be fitting into their lifestyles as it is more regressive than progressive in so many ways.

Critical Thinking

I have used in this book an outlook of critical thinking in defining concepts, using theoretical reasoning for discussing selected issues, deciding the use of particular methodology for empirical study of each topic at hand, and interpreting my research findings. I must say that critical thinking helped me in becoming meaningful in my discussions.

Numerous interpretations of critical thinking as to what it is or is not have appeared in the literature. Overall, my use of critical thinking in this book implies a goal oriented and systematically articulated thought process based on selected criteria or attributes. Many of these criteria I selected have often been traditionally used in the literature[6] and are briefly summarized below in four paragraphs.

(a) Comprehensive Assessment

Critical thinking does not imply here any narrow or parochial outlook. It seeks an overall understanding of the phenomena in broader context even if it is focused on a specific topic. This style of thinking looks carefully at all options and alternatives for seeking explanation, prediction, and prevention of a social issue such as terrorism. It avoids causal linkages among variables particularly in social phenomena. For example, it would not be valid for someone to say that "religious fanaticism is the major cause of a suicide attack" on the basis of data that are not based on a seriously planned temporal sequence of variables. I will carefully avoid any form of causal linkages, reductionism, oversimplification, determinism, and overgeneralization in reaching any conclusion in this book. I will make statements only in a conditional sense based on probability. I will employ a notion of "multiple levels of analysis"[7] (for example, [a] physical/ecological, [b] individual or psychological, [c] cultural or institutional, and [d] social or interactional) for presenting explanations and discussions in several of my chapters.

(b) Objective and Scientific Approach

Critical thinking requires that I avoid judgmental statements based on any form of subjectivity, prejudice, discrimination, and labeling. As indicated earlier in the Preface, I will not even name any specific religions or denominations, specific countries, and historical data in my discussions. Reference to these based on selected literature will be noted only in the endnotes for each chapter. I will keep the main text of my book free of specific events and geographical locations so I can largely focus on issues involved. In addition, I will base several of my main presentations in the book based on empirical data that I have been collecting during the past several years while developing several conceptual ideas. My book may interest people of multiple religious and cultural backgrounds as I stay neutral and take no side to any particular ideology. I will avoid making conclusive statements and will generally imply conditional statements based on the notion of probability. Nor will I mean to be judgmental in my discussions of quite controversial topics. My major goal in the book is to contribute toward developing ideas on serious forms of violence and their prevention. I do have some preferences on certain positions related to these topics. I just want to express ideas based on a general understanding of issues involved rather than becoming emotionally involved in taking sides as I find done in several publications around.

(c) Conceptual Thinking

Conceptual thinking, unlike descriptive thinking, is analytical and logical way of developing ideas and addressing problems. It is based on theoretical reasoning and rational logic. For example, theoretical reasoning will involve the use of some theoretical frame of reference as well as a realistic and not blind-faith logic for developing and interpreting empirical data as well as ideas relevant to an issue at hand. The theoretical reasoning plays a role in providing clues to deeper meanings of ideas as well as concepts used. I will define all major concepts (such as religion, religiosity, fanaticism, rationality, secularism, non-violence, and so forth) before using them in discussions.

(d) Constructive Reasoning

Critical thinking does not involve emotional excitement, sensationalism, doom and gloom ideologies, overall attitude of negativism, and arbitrary skepticism. I will uphold a positive outlook in identifying preventive strategies providing a sense of promise for resolving the problem. In my view, that may help us deal with fear of terrorism instead of generating pessimistic perspective that is often desired by terrorists to begin with. While baseless optimism and overstated idealism may generate false consciousness[8] and ineffectiveness, a cautiously articulated outlook of prevention may help us build hope and promise through action rather than giving up in vain. It is of course important that we develop preventive strategies for terrorist events in the future through rational or realistic logic rather than mere formula type wish lists based on some fantasies.

THEORETICAL PERSPECTIVES USED

A theoretical perspective provides us a way of 'looking and interpreting' whatever we study. A theoretical reasoning helps us in providing clues to deeper meanings in our thought processes. I am not particularly sold on any particular theory and use in the book an eclectic approach for selecting whichever perspective helps me to understand any given issue. I do want to mention that many of the theoretical perspectives in all natural and social sciences may have had linkages to metaphysics, including philosophy and theology. However, more and more contemporary theories in all sciences are being developed on research than on metaphysics.

I am briefly stating meanings of four theoretical orientations used under various titles and interpretations in social sciences, including sociology.[9] I am aware that there are many other approaches using different titles. I am choosing the following four as the major ones that have helped me to understand issues and concepts addressed in this book.

Realism Oriented Conflict Perspective

This theoretical approach recognizes realities of inequalities, violence and conflicts in human society.[10] It uses a rather confrontational as well as critical approach in studying realities of terrorism. It denounces violence based on any form of hate, racism, religious background, and class differences (for example, exploitation of the masses by the ruling elite resulting in the alienation of the former). Conflicts in society or within the individual's personality have to be dealt with rather than be ignored or repressed.

The conflict theory will be instrumental in understanding processes in the book, particularly chapters dealing with the analysis of violence typologies and terrorism.

Idealistic Perspective

Ideology dealing with any topic of legitimate interest consists of a scheme of ideas on the topic generally oriented toward philosophical interpretations.[11] Examples of ideologies in the relevant literature include the so-called 'enlightenment' movements after industrial and urban revolutions. These include, among others, such titles as capitalism, democracy, positivism, rationalism, reformation, and humanism. The ideological reasoning is justified on such grounds as promoting political or economic movements of change during the 17th century followed later with advancement in progressive ideas by the Renaissance thinkers in the 19th century. These movements of thought seriously looked for ideas that would improve society and its institutions including government and religion. That is why such idealistic ideas were considered as parts of the new age of reason.

An ideology may set ideal moral standards to aspire for. The ideology of, for example, "Justice for All" so prominently used in the American system of justice underlines an outlook for courts and criminal justice officials. I always tell my students not to worry about the problems involved in actually applying all the way that notion in the administration of justice as it is unreal in a practical sense to be able to treat all people always 'equal' in legal situations. Instead, we may want to consider the notion aimed at setting an ideal standard for the law enforcement people to aspire for even if they may not be fully able to achieve its goal involved. In that sense, ideologies are justified to set our goals in society we can aspire for.

Functionalism theory in sociology has emphasis on the institutionalization and the normative order that keep the social system functioning. For example, while discussing the relevance or the use of the institution of religion in the process of violence in various forms, I will touch in Chapter 6 on advantages or functions of that institution in human society. I will also explore the constructive idealism of 'secularism' in Chapter 7 and of 'non-violence' in Chapter 8.

Rational Perspective

Rationalism and individualism oriented perspective on utilitarianism and behaviorist psychology made significant contribution to psychological issues as well as political and economic discussions particularly in the 19th century.[12] Exchange theory[13] provided an in-depth analysis of the importance of rational outlook and a sense of 'distributive justice' and reciprocity in human relations. In addition, rationalism · emphasizes the importance of reason and pragmatic bases of social behaviors and leadership[14] and added new dimensions and potentials for analyzing and assessing costs and outcomes of human conduct including violence and terrorism. I will be referring to rationality implications in dealing with terrorcide, religiosity, secularism, non-violence, and other conceptualizations in the book.

Social Psychological Perspective

Social scientists, including some in psychology and sociology, have been advocating needs for comprehensively analyzing social issues by incorporating several levels and dimensions of those issues for understanding and explaining them.[15] In addition, this perspective interprets the individual's personality or mental health as a process and not a 'completed' outcome or a 'finished product' as such.[16] Many working in the area of health, for example, are going beyond a 'medical' model incorporating dimensions such as what is experienced and perceived by the individual at the phenomenological level of reality. There has been an increasing awareness about a traditionally maintained somewhat meaningless distinction between 'physical health' and 'mental health' and instead for considering a holistic phenomenon of total health. Likewise, social scientists are increasingly avoiding the usage of labels and profiles for the so-called 'criminals' and 'terrorists' by only identifying probable characteristics or attributes of behaviors relevant to issues and problems. It seems that the labeling approach is rapidly becoming outdated for understanding and preventing social problems.

In this book, I attempt to understand violence and terrorisms as multi-dimensional concepts analyzed through typologies and characteristic as components of concepts identified in different chapters in this book (see methodology used for them stated below) are done at multiple levels of analysis.[17]

DEVELOPING TYPOLOGIES AND CHARACTERISTICS

I developed the following 'historical' and 'classificatory' typologies,[18] classifications, categorizations, and selected profiling characteristics relevant to various concepts and phenomena relevant in the book. I constructed them through the Delphi procedures.

(a) Types of violence and associated personality characteristics, behaviors, and attitudes identified in Chapter 2.

(b) Characteristics of terrorism presented in Chapter 3.

(c) A typology of suicide terrorism ('Terrorcide') presented in Chapter 4.

(d) Profiling characteristics of terrorists and terrorciders discussed in Chapter 5.

(e) Characteristics of fanaticism as conceptualized in Chapter 6.

(f) Preventive strategies for terrorism presented in Chapter 7.

(g) Characteristics of secularism outlined in Chapter 7.

(h) Types of non-violence principles and associated indicators, including the assertiveness scale conceptualized in Chapter 8.

Usefulness of the Delphi Technique

The Delphi approach has been used in studies concerning several kinds of problem areas especially as a tool for planning and forecasting. It has proved to be a valuable technique for planning and forecasting the long-term future.[19] Several studies sponsored by the Rand Corporation are known to have employed Delphi procedures for developing criteria for decision-making and policy formulation.[20]

A number of scholars have discussed the merits of the Delphi approach. I am summarizing a few of them below:

(1) The Delphi approach relies on the rationality of group judgment, or "n-heads are better than one". It is a process of eliciting and refining the opinions of a group of individuals. The individuals remain anonymous to each other; their opinions are continually refined and reiterated; and feedback to participants is privatized and controlled.

(2) The Delphi approach is a variant of the panel or committee approach for arriving at a consensus of majority opinions. Its design eliminates or prevents face-to-face confrontation, specious persuasion, and the bandwagon effect of a majority agreement. It replaces direct discussion with a series of carefully controlled questionnaires that report back edited and new information to the participants, where they act in privacy and react to the successive inputs.

(3) The Delphi approach uses some form of statistical index as a representative of the group opinion. Thus, there is no particular attempt to arrive at unanimity among the respondents, and a spread of opinions on the final round is the normal outcome.

(4) The Delphi approach is very useful in such areas as exploring development of typologies and components of concepts that will eventually lead to additional research for their further testing and verification. This 'intuitive technique' utilizes the knowledge of experts in a particular area of concern for at least making a beginning in issues needing attention.

(5) The Delphi approach provides flexibility for the research in various ways. There is no 'cut and dried' set of steps to follow and it provides variations of possibilities during each phase of inquiry.

Four Steps in the Delphi Procedures

The methodology for developing each of the nine concepts and their components listed earlier in the chapter consisted of the Delphi procedures. The Delphi technique has methodological potentials for utilizing the knowledge of experts in a particular area of investigation. The Delphi procedures for developing a list of characteristics of each topic consisted of the following four steps:

1. Developing Initial List of the Components of a Concept

First, I conducted a comprehensive review of the literature and a content analysis of the secondary data from various sources relevant to each of the nine topics mentioned in the list stated earlier in this chapter. Second, based on that review and content analysis, I identified a list of characteristics, behaviors, and components of the topic (for example, secularism) based on the existing knowledge after conducting the said review. The major step toward accomplishing that objective was to prepare an initial list of characteristics of the topic or concept that could be handed over to experts or judges who would rank them in terms of degree of importance and then also could add, if they choose, other items to that list whatever additional characteristic(s) considered being relevant by them to the topic.

2. Selection of Experts or Judges

Second, I selected a 'panel of experts or judges' consisting of faculty members in social sciences and humanities (having a background in several disciplines, such as anthropology, criminology, law enforcement, jurisprudence, education, psychology, forensics, business, history, religion, political science, economics, social work, and sociology) in the area universities and colleges, journalists in prominent news media in nearby urban communities, public officials working in agencies relevant to a given topic, and known community and political leaders in the region who were assumed to be knowledgeable of the topic and related issues. The experts were selected through a snow-balling or chain-referral technique based upon their reputation and interest in the field.

Thus, I started with a short list of prominent persons in each category and asked each of them to give me names of knowledgeable or interested persons in the topic concerned, when possible. I was able to identify 32 to 93 names of these potential respondents in nine different surveys and collected my data from as many of them as possible. The non-random sample in my studies (reported in this book in various chapters) during the past six years was justified because of the exploratory nature of my research.

3. Interviewing the Respondents

Third, I contacted and personally interviewed respondents through a questionnaire consisting of conceptually related components of each of the nine topics that had been identified earlier through the first step consisting of review of literature and secondary data. Interviewing respondents appeared to be a necessity for me because of the sensitive nature of topics as well as the types of respondents involved. In addition, interviewing respondents ensured a satisfactory response rate and I took notes on their candid reactions to items and their comments helped me in evaluating their responses.

4. Analyzing and Interpreting Findings

Fourth, I statistically analyzed responses from the first round of interviews to determine the degree of consensus among respondents on each item of the profile. Then, in a second round, I provided them with their average responses (mean, standard deviation, and interquartile range) on each item from the first round and asked them to reconsider their earlier responses if considered necessary by them. The standard deviation on an item represented a degree of consensus among respondents, while a mean response on the scale was an indicator of the degree of an item's importance in relation to other items. I assumed that in cases where a person's response is outside the group interquartile range, justification for the extreme response was requested by me for clarification during the second round.

I will be reporting summary of findings based on my surveys in various chapters of the book.

CONCLUDING REMARKS

Chapter 1 identifies objectives and justification for work on this book and its contents. It should provide the readers an overview of how I approached the subject matter in the book differently as compared to other books on terrorism. I clarified my global and critical thinking outlook on the subject. I pointed out the theoretical and methodological approaches used in discussing and interpreting my subject matter. This chapter hopefully provides you an overview of the book's contents and its expected contribution in making presentations in the remaining nine chapters.

Chapters 2, 3 and 4 will provide you a conceptual background to understanding violence, terrorism, and terrorcide, followed by Chapters 5 and 6 that identify selected explanations and consequences of terrorism, and, finally, Chapters 7 and 8 closing with positive or constructive notes on preventing the problem of that form of violence into the future.

2

Reality and Types of Violence

The theory of natural selection is grounded on the belief that each new variety, and ultimately each new species, is produced and maintained by having some advantage over those with which it comes into competition; and the consequent extinction of less-favored forms almost inevitably follows.

—Charles Darwin

The tendency to aggression is an innate, independent, instinctual disposition in man...it constitutes the powerful obstacle to culture.

—Sigmund Freud

Violence is not the only form of power. Sometimes it is the least effective. Always it is the most vicious, for the perpetrator as well as for the victim.

—Howard Zinn

Violence (himsa) degrades and corrupts man, to meet force with force and hatred with hatred only increases man's progressive degeneration. Violent policies have not only proved bankrupt but threaten man with extinction.

—Mahatma Gandhi

MEANING AND TYPES OF VIOLENCE

Violence in this book is understood as something that is done to a person or persons. We should distinguished between the doing of violence and merely acting violently: a frenzied lunatic might act violently; he would not be doing violence, though perhaps acting violently can be similar to, and the potential it implies for, the doing of violence.[1] I have listed in Table 2.1 selected examples of behaviors and attitudes under three types of violent tendencies identified and ranked in importance by selected experts in my research through Delphi procedures that were described in Chapter 1.

Table 2.1: Examples of Personality Characteristics, Behaviors and Attitudes Under Three Aspects of Violence

Violent Tendencies	Personality Characteristics/Behaviors/Attitudes
1. Hostility	• angry; furious; intolerant; impatient; rude; impolite; battlefield mentality • destructive; killing; advocating weaponry; toughness; brutality; savagery; rampage; severity; turbulence • anxious; intense; stressful; outraged; infuriated; upset; antagonistic; restless; belligerent; berserk; bickering; tense; rebellious; zealot; opposes diversity and looks for adversity • harassing; insulting; distrustful; invasive; unfriendly • harassing; insulting; distrustful; exaggerating; hateful; maladjusted
2. Dominance	• threatening; mighty; generates fear • control freak; seeks expansion of power; oppressive; authoritarian; glamorize past dictators • believes in invasion/attacking/aggression; militant; combative; intrusive; assaultive; coercive; cruel • force-surrender oriented • defeating; wanting to win/prevail; conquering; repressive • being in-charge; ruling; commanding; dictating • interested in governing-regulating • exploiting; enslaving
3. Irrationality	• radical; fanatic; extremist; determinist; fundamentalist; bigot; literalist; anarchist; criminal minded • mad; paranoid; bipolar; emotionally obsessed/disturbed; impulsive-compulsive • arrogant; egotistical; intolerant; demanding; lawless

	• prejudiced; discriminatory • revengeful; vindictive; goes for an eye for an eye • inflexible/rigid; likes selective change • emotionally aroused; rationalizes errors and aggression • believes in end justifying means • selfish; greedy; manipulative; uncaring; unforgiving

Thus, as indicated in Table 2.1, violent behaviors and attitudes in my definition of doing violence include at least some degree of (i) hostility, (ii) dominance, and (iii) irrationality. My definition of violence may be relatively broader than several scholarly definitions that basically state: "violence is the infliction of injury or suffering on someone." The World Health Organization's 1996 definition is quite comprehensive: "Violence is defined as the intentional use of physical force or power, threatened or actual, against oneself, another person, or against a group or community, that either results in or has a high likelihood of resulting in injury, death, psychological harm, maldevelopment or deprivation."[2]

My definition goes beyond a judgment, made on the bases of moral or normative values in society, about the consequence of a 'violent' behavior or attitude. It incorporates the idea that violence is both manifest and latent as a process involving hostility, dominance, and irrational behaviors regardless of whether it has caused injury or suffering to others. I also contend that an identification of motive is not essential to the analysis of violence. Whether someone 'meant' to actually or accidentally hurt other(s) is unimportant. If certain incidents are called as 'negligent' (i.e., involving failure to show due caution or care that results in an injury or harm), or legally defined as 'reckless' (i.e., acting in such a manner as to greatly increase the potential for injury), they may still be considered to be *violent* as per my definition. What is important is that the violent person possesses some of the behavioral or attitudinal traits toward victims stated in Table 2.1. Victims may include an individual, a group of people, a collectivity (e.g., a nation or a community). Victims may be humans and/or animals, including their property.

My inclusion of irrationality and dominant orientations as components of the definition of violence may underline or imply some type or degree of emotionally disturbed state in the violent person whereby he/she loses control over social acts, hostile attitudes and tendencies. As shown in the next chapter, I find this definition meaningful in discussing violence as a terrorist behavior or outlook.

I am stating below two scenarios or cases to illustrate complexities in defining violence in real life.

Case #1. Mr. XYZ baby sits a ten months old female child as her mother goes for shopping. He sexually molests/rapes the child causing serious injuries, gets arrested, tried in court, and found guilty of a 'lesser' crime called 'sexual assault' on child. The prosecutor tried conviction for rape but failed because the country where this case took place had a rape law requiring that "for rape to occur the victim's 'sense of chastity' must be hurt by the sexual act". Since a ten month old girl "did not yet have a sense of chastity", the offender did not rape.

Case #2. A father occasionally helped his daughter take bath and usually stayed in the bathroom shaving or brushing his teeth while she was in the bath tub. As she passed age 6 or so, she started locking bathroom door wanting some privacy. Her father got angry because his 'little girl' had stopped trusting him as a father by refusing to allow his presence in the bathroom when she took bath. After a complaint was filed by mother, the state prosecutor filed sexual abuse charge against father and won the case because the court ruled that the bottom line definition of sexual abuse of a child is her/his 'perception' of abuse rather than whether it was 'meant' or not. Assuming that the father was *actually* innocent and did not *mean* to harass his daughter, the bottom line still was some form of violence occurred as perceived by the victim. The father should have been aware that his little girl now was a little grown up and had developed a self concept resulting in some fear or shyness in undressing in front of him as a parent.

Legitimacy of Violence

Violence is a human universal; no human society is known where some degree and certain forms of violent acts are absent. In some ways, various violent acts (such as wars and other forms of aggressions) have been institutionalized in human history on the bases of laws and security policies. However, it may be asserted that violence in human society is a non-legitimate phenomenon.[3] The definition of violence stated above is based on the notion that violence may be arbitrarily legitimized or rationalized; it would be difficult to rationally and realistically justify it unless you do so through the so-called 'rational self interest theory'. That theory has actually misguided social scientists shifting attention from prevention to punishment. To consider that violence is 'rational' and dictated by 'self interest' can only blind us to the reality of those forms of violence and passionate rage that have been most horrendously destructive of human life around the word.[4]

In some ways, violence can be interpreted as a symptom of psychopathology at the individual level and anomie (normlessness) at the social level. At best, it is a deviant phenomenon contributing only to dysfunctioning of the individuals as well as social disruptions and disorganization. Violence sometimes is considered to be rational for short-term goals and at times legitimized by certain customs or traditions and even selective interpretations of laws. It does not, however, promote causes, neither history nor progress.[5]

The possibility of the legitimacy of violence may be considered through its 'relativity' in regard to a context, individuals, or culture involved. For example, the violence of soldier against an enemy soldier in an institutionalized war is, except to the most adamant pacifist, considered legitimate. The violence of victim against criminal in moments of self-defense is legitimate. The violence of lion against the zebra is probably legitimate in nature.[6] Relativism tells us that what is considered 'wrong' in one situation or cultural context may be 'right' in another. However, as will be discussed further in Chapter 8, the ideology of violence in human society is unjustified but may be rationalized by people in various contexts. Violence, therefore, may be often found to be:

- Non-legitimate, wrongful use of force, and pathological but an essential part of reality of life/nature;
- Momentary or a temporary phase, or it may become enduring, lasting or even a permanent condition or way of life of an individual and in a given culture/society;
- Universal or generalized trend (such as in the entertainment industry, including certain sports and games) or it may be localized, individualized, context dependent and unique historical condition; and
- A condition and a process that needs to be carefully researched and understood so we can meet challenges of resolving its complex impacts thereby minimizing the hurt (particularly perceived by the victim) resulting from it.

Categories of Violence

A number of categories of violence have been addressed in the literature. A few examples are stated below:

- Self-directed violence refers to self-inflicted abuse, mutilation, chronic addiction or substance abuse, and suicide attempts/completion.
- Collective violence, such as terrorism, on the other hand, is directed at generalized others, communities, or particular groups of people.
- Interpersonal or the so-called intimate/family violence is directed at children, spouses, and the elderly.
- Media violence, which is exposure to violence through popular media, such as television shows, movies, video games, music and print.[7]
- Natural violence refers to the violence in nature based on inherent and spontaneous tendencies that are predictable. It is considered to be 'normal' violence found, for example, among animals. Violence among

human beings has complex motives and is not as predictable.

Degree of Violence

There seems to be a variety of styles, forms, and levels of what violence is, where a behavior starts from cool and mild anger to serious levels of anxiety, stress, hostilities, and obsession of destruction and violence. We are talking about a range of violent tendencies from "normal neurosis of relatively adjusted people with manageable or routine anger and anxiety"[8] to highly disturbed, authoritarian and psychotic people ready to blow-up and are aggressively planning for engaging in mass killings.[9] We will address the use of religious fanaticism by the latter type of hostile people in Chapter 6 of this book.

Discussions have occurred in scientific works as well as philosophical literature attempting to conclude as to which species have higher degrees of violence than others. My conclusion from those discussions is that while there are significant differences in styles and types of violence found among various species, it is extremely difficult to rank them in any hierarchical order from most violent to most peaceful, unless we do that arbitrarily based on our own judgment. Same way, we cannot really imply any type of 'superiority' or 'inferiority' of status of various species involved in the Darwinian notion of the "survival of the fittest"[10] either. Darwin's notion of 'fitness' was based on the degree of adaptability any species has in comparison to others in the process of the "struggle for existence".[11] Thus, Darwin's notion of the 'dominant' species was based on its survivability and not any form of superiority as such. Darwin did write: "Man in the rudest state in which he now exists is the most dominant animal that has appeared on this earth. He has spread more widely than any other organized form and all others have yielded before him. He manifestly owes his immense superiority to his intellectual faculties...."[12] In fact, however, it is only some of us human beings who have been implying some level of own superiority based on, for example, some belief systems advocating a special origin of us as a species. Undoubtedly, we human beings may have appearance of the 'dominant' species on earth and beyond based on our selected biological and intelligence capabilities enabling us achieve a 'higher' degree of adaptability and control over other species in some ways. For example, beginning with the primitive capacity for defensive behavior, humans may have evolved several adaptive functions from it. "Indeed, early man was not basically biologically adapted as a predator, and he has only become one secondarily by the use of tools or technology created through his intelligence. We, therefore, arrive at a picture of primitive man, not as a fierce, dangerous, and constantly aggressive individual but rather as a relatively small, slight, and fearful being, finding safety only in groups, sometimes being called upon to act bravely, but actually inflicting damage only when extremely fearful."[13]

Philosophers and social scientists also add to this by stating that human beings as a species also have been social, compassionate, and basically cooperative with fellow beings despite of engagement by some in deviant and violent episodes. Certain violent activities seem to have become rather dangerous for us as well as for our planet for our future survival. Overall, therefore, the judgment on idealizing ourselves as some type of 'superior' species is irrelevant in realizing our realities. Of course, I take a constructive view of us for our adaptability and survival in the last three chapters in the book.

FACTORS RELATED TO VIOLENCE

I will identify the explanation of violence in terms for various factors as correlates (causality not implied) to some of the violent tendencies and behaviors in general (as correlates may be different in various types and forms of violence) stated earlier in Table 2.1. The factors are identified at various levels of analysis mentioned earlier in Chapter 1. By doing so, I hope to provide you a broader view of understanding some background to various aspects of the process of violence in human society. Correlates of terrorism in particular are discussed in Chapter 5.

Ecological Factors

Physical environmental factors have been found to be associated to temperament including aggressive behaviors among animals.[14] One of the most important factors found to be correlated to violence among animals as well as humans has been the size and density of population where they live. For example, large size and dense populations in major cities lead to serious conflicts and competition among people. Rural sociologists have found people residing in county side are generally more intimate and friendly as compared to those as urban dwellers.[15] It seems that in congested environments people tend to develop social distance, irritability, and negative attitudes toward each other as if they get on each others' nerves.

Biological Factors

Biological theories of violence concentrate on the physical substrate of our nature and behaviors. This substrate includes our brain, our body, our chemistry, and our genes. Darwinists who readily exploited their ideas developed the following assumptions for the evolutionary process: (1) the evolutionary processes of natural selection and the survival of the fittest applied to the development of races, nations, and empires; (2) war and violence constituted necessary tests or proving grounds of nation's fitness to survive; and (3) on these assumptions, social Darwinists prescribed the incalculation of warrior like virtues, physical fitness, and war-readiness as vital conditions for national, racial, and imperial survival. In addition, Lorenz argued that human aggression is a basic organic drive or instinct as vital for man's basic physiological needs as the drives of hunger and sex. Lorenz believed that intraspecific human aggression has gone wild and become a danger to man's survival. No matter what the specific emphasis of the theory, biological explanations look for what is 'wrong with' the violent individual in terms of his or her physical characteristics.[16] The medical model of mental health looks for sources of anxiety and depression in biochemical changes in human body. Scientists have connected the shape and size of the body to anti-social behaviors, including violence. Chemical and hormonal imbalances have been connected to mental as well as physical illnesses. The electroconvulsive therapy and lobotomy of the brain have been used in the past for treating aggressive behaviors.

Significant heredity and breeding differences have been found among humans and animals. Gender or sex differences, for example, have been significant in relation to anger and violence.[17] Males generally are known to exhibit violent behaviors and attitudes more significantly than females. A commonly known reason for males being relatively more aggressive is stated by some studies stating that males have more testosterone than females.[18] Interestingly, the most serious violence tends to be committed by males against males that are not in their sexually receptive state.[19] I will address additional details on gender differences in violence related to cultural and social factors later in this chapter.

Psychological Factors

While the biological factors emphasize the origin of violence to being inherent in human beings, the psychological perspective considers it as a personality disorder that develops through learning and other micro-level sources.[20] One of the leading figures focusing on the deviant nature of human personality was Sigmund Freud. He conceived the central elements of personality to consist of the id, the ego, and the superego, the id taking over many of the phenomena of the original unconscious self and the superego being the societal sensor. His recognition of the 'hidden nature of man' having potentials produce inner conflicts and stressors leading to violent tendencies. He particularly elaborated in his work on *Civilization and Its Discontent* how the contemporary human being has learnt to have a life of frustrations and contradictions along with destructive urges for own self as well as others.[21] Several other personality theories beside that of Freud have conducted a great deal of research on sources and impacts of violence. In addition, behaviorist work (for example, by Skinner) on conditioning has interesting applications concerning the problem of human aggression.

Another example of a psychological interpretation of violence is referred to as the strain theory as well as the so-called aggression-frustration perspective.[22] The theory emphasizes how certain stresses and strains people experience increase the likelihood of violence in their lives. Various forms of strains (stresses, anxieties and frustrations) upset individuals, developing relative deprivations, thereby creating pressure for corrective action. Some individuals may respond in a violent manner, with violence being used to reduce strain and/or obtain revenge against the source of strain or related targets.

Sociocultural Factors

I briefly summarized in Chapter 1 four sociological approaches (conflict theory, functionalism, exchange-rational perspective, and social-psychological interactionism) relevant to interpreting human violence. Based on a philosophical background from Hegel, Malthus, Darwin, and Marx, the conflict approach recognizes violence as a reality based on stresses from inequalities and injustices in human society. Violence, therefore, has to be dealt with rather than be suppressed or denied. Functionalist idealism, like control theory, on the other hand, advocates a social management of conflicts and violence as they are disruptive to the functioning of social system. Exchange outlook has a pragmatic approach to dealing with violence through, for example, negotiation and conciliations for identifying ways of adjusting and dealing with violence. The interactional perspective is somewhat eclectic in approaching violence through analyses at both social and psychological levels. I will be elaborating these theories in Chapter 5 while dealing with an explanation of terrorism. I will also be outlining in that chapter selected sociocultural factors correlated to violence in general and terrorism in particular.

CONCLUDING REMARKS

I needed to provide you an overview of violence as a conceptual background to terrorism which is our focus in this book. Violence and its dimensions/characteristics are too complex to summarize in a short chapter. I at least defined the way and in whatever sense I am using the notion relevant to the book's theme. Additional details relevant to violence will be incorporated in several of the following chapters.

3

Terrorism: The Dirty Violence

It's not the bullet with my name on it that worries me.
It's the one that says 'To whom it may concern'.

—Anonymous Belfast resident,
quoted in *London Guardian*, 1991

Some studies have noted that terrorism is on the rise in numbers as well as in significance of impact despite serious efforts made by various countries for controlling or even combating it.[1] In addition, it appears that the problem of terrorism has added newer and more dangerous forms of violence against people, including methods or tactics such as so-called 'suicide terrorism' and the carefully planned use of religion for recruiting and training terrorists.[2] The potential for as well as incidents of terrorism in today's world have not only increased but have also become relatively more aggressive, truly global conducted by transnational and non-state actors. These individuals are well-financed, difficult to penetrate, and have increased access to creative technology and all sorts of weapons of destruction.[3] The present chapter is devoted to identifying meanings, styles and forms of terrorism as a movement involving serious violence in contemporary societies.

CHARACTERISTICS OF TERRORISM

Literature on terrorism has been abundant, and still increasing in a diverse coverage, examining critically various forms of this phenomenon. Undoubtedly, it is not easy to define terrorism because of its multiple meanings in research studies as well as in applied fields, including governmental leaderships and security/intelligence agencies and the military in various countries. There is not a set definition of terrorism that has gained universal acceptance. Terrorism does not seem to be a systematically developed ideology. It may be an approach or method used by some people for achieving some goal that is probably perceived by them to be beneficial regardless of its destructive outcome for society. A research paper in a recent reader on terrorism just concluded that only few terms or concepts in political discourse have proved as hard to define as terrorism.[4] Definitions differ in terms of those legally developed by various governments across the globe, intelligence and security agencies, and so-considered experts and scientists. Meanings of the term range from individual terrorists to guerilla warfare. However, while this may not be a problem for rhetorical purposes,[5] it is important that we have a definition to identify at least some characteristics of the phenomenon to be able to assess its magnitude, correlates, and consequences.

New focus in recent studies has identified multiple motives, threats, goals, and means or strategies in defining terrorism.[6] Other studies have been going over multiple challenges in conceptualizing this form of violence. These include people defining the concept differently in multiple contexts.[7] For example, one study restricts the meaning of terrorism to violence at non-combatants mainly for political purposes to instill fear among them and extort, intimidate, or coerce them to change.[8] However, a consensus has been developing in recent literature on the subject on defining terrorism as the use or threatened use of violence mainly for political goals.[9] My definition is oriented to that direction using the components of violence spelled out in Chapter 2.

Characteristics of terrorism, stated in Table 3.1, are based on both its extensity (in terms of how widespread it is) and its intensity (in terms of its impact which is spelled out in Chapter 5). I will first discuss characteristics and then summarize notes on typologies. I identified a number of behavioral characteristics and attitudes of violence and violent people in

Chapter 2. Most of those listed there seem to apply to people engaging in terrorism.

Table 3.1: Characteristics and Types of Terrorism

Characteristics of Terrorism	Types of Terrorism
1. A Serious and Distinct Form of Violence 2. Cause Driven Form of Violence 3. Whether Terrorist Missions Adequately Planned 4. Whether Terrorist Missions Use/Abuse Established Institutions 5. Emphasis on Covert Operations 6. Terrorism: A Dirty Violence 7. Goals and Methods Used for Recruitment and Training of Terrorists 8. Degree of Disregard to Civilian Injuries	• Regionally Centered • International/Global • Focused on Separatist Groups • Religious Terrorism • Retributional Terrorists • Ethno-Nationalist Terrorism • Anarchist Terrorism • Right-Wing Terrorism • Left-Wing Terrorism • State-sponsored Terrorism and Insurgency • Demonstrative Terrorism • Narco Terrorism • Cyber Terrorism • Mass Destruction Terrorism

I am enumerating now selected additional characteristics of terrorist movements as serious forms of violence. These characteristics were identified through a review of relevant literature and then were selected and ranked in degree of importance by experts in my research project based on the Delphi procedures as described earlier in Chapter 1.

Terrorism: A Serious and Distinct Form of Violence

Terrorism may be considered as an important and, if not unique all the way, a distinct form of serious violence against humanity. It is so because of its impact, some of that is illustrated to some degree in Chapter 7. It is likely not be an ordinary or day-to-day incident of violence such as experienced by children in schools, or by spouses in family, or by minorities in ethnic relations. Domestic violence or murders are not terrorism because the goal is to kill or murder specific persons, rather than targeting a random and significant civilian population. As an example, a man who did not want his wife to leave him may kill his wife. It is very unlikely that he will begin bombing civilians until his wife agrees to stay with him. These types of violence also do not qualify to be terrorism because they are not aimed at coercing the government into acquiescing to demands.

Terrorists are seen as psychopathic individuals having religious or political cause.[10] It is an extreme, cruel, merciless, obsessed, and sneaky form of violence, legitimize irrational goals.

Terrorism is loaded with hostility, sense of dominance, and irrationality illustrated in Chapter 2. Terrorism is a sort of hate crime, full of anger and revenge. It perhaps goes beyond a murder or rape committed at a local level because its impact has often national and even global in many instances. In fact, there is no substantial theoretical literature in social science that can cover the uniqueness of the terrorist phenomena.[11]

Cause Driven Form of Violence

Terrorism is generally driven by outrageous goals that may seldom be realistic or achievable. The goals may be set with an outlook of "ends are justified without consideration for available means" as if the outlook for an end is *absolute* in meaning. Once the goal is set by a terrorist or an organization, it is unquestionable and is justified in its own right; no discussions for its viability may be considered. Revolutionary violence, anarchists, freedom fighters, and separatists have known for disregarding principles and ground rules of warfare.[12] Terrorists, on the other hand, usually want submission and control ascribing the importance of symbolism for their actions. The so-called 'new terrorism' is well financed, internationally located, difficult to penetrate to stop its spread, continuously recruiting for ambitious goals, and safety from it cannot be taken for granted.

Whether Terrorist Missions Adequately Planned

Means for achieving a terrorist goal may be often set arbitrarily without careful planning. The planning may often be based on achieving a goal in the short run rather than assessing outcomes for the long haul. As such, terrorists execute planned campaigns that aim to destroy as much property and life as possible, thereby forcing the government to capitulate. Without these parameters, a violent act is not terrorism. Terrorist missions may occasionally be committed and mission focused on achieving a specific goal but they may not always be a part of larger conspiracy and may often be localized making impact in bits and pieces in relatively small scales. However, their obscure operations are unpredictable and there are always going to be fears that they use weapons of massive impacts at the global level. Since their leadership is often fluid and changing, their overall impact on our secure world remains indefinite.

Whether Terrorist Missions Use/Abuse Established Institutions

Institutional support for terrorist missions is generally use for the purpose of legitimating their activities. Terrorists are often known for abusing political, governmental, economic, and social institutions established through traditions and some even rational grounds. I will address, for example, the use of religion in some terrorist actions in Chapter 6. Several terrorist movements and projects also have political goals or connections. For example, quite few of the terrorist incidents have been linked to the so-called 'separatist' movements claiming independent statehood or a political identity. Some terrorist acts may be linked to 'leftist' or 'rightist' ideologies often based on their opportunistic outlook fitting particular missions involved.

Emphasis on Covert Operations

Many terrorist individuals or groups tend to make-believe in being covert, underground, or secretive operation. However, some adopt a name, a theme, or identity linked to a slogan such as being 'freedom fighters' pursuing a just cause or some humanistic goal. Generally, they stay obscure and ambiguous by hiding actual goals, may have double standards, and mysterious so that they can change strategies suiting each mission and its outcome. Many of them thrive on misinformation and deceit.[13]

Terrorism: A Dirty Violence

Terrorism is generally based on unjust and arbitrarily rationalized goals. It is termed as a 'dirty' form of warfare because its operation is not really institutionalized as such. Using other institutions such as religion does not qualify this form of violence to be termed as an institution as such. This form of violence is arbitrary, has no rational basis, and any clearly defined normative structure. Comparing it other forms of violence such as the institution of war would not be legitimate. For example, it is said that during a major war,[14] the opposing armies would lay down their arms at dusk, help the injured of both parties, have supper together before moving to their respective tents, and enter the battle ground again at dawn to fight. Actions of violence in regular warfare are expected to be systematically institutionalized, often through internationally established principles. Terrorists, on the other hand, basically desire publicity on infliction of injury and damage, often assassinate people ruthlessly, make political and innocent captives as hostages, and use extreme measures to achieve whatever goals.

For a 'just cause' of war, the following criteria are to be met:[15]

- There must be significant hostility from the enemy or the country is under attack; non-violence solutions must be hopeless;
- The war is legally declared by the enemy;
- Going to war must be the last resort; and
- There must be a reasonable hope to win.

Just means in warfare:

- Do not overkill;
- Intend no harm to innocent people; and
- Take the hit but complete the mission.

Finally, terrorists are not known to be inventive and mostly used older types of weaponry in their arsenals, relying on bombs and bullets. Yet they seem to have demonstrated a great deal of ingenuity in terms of tactics in the selection of means or methods and in timing of violence to cause maximum damage.

Goals and Methods Used for Recruitment and Training of Terrorists

Among national and transnational terrorist groups, the most crucial areas of cooperation is in the recruitment and training sectors. As a result of the commonalities in sociological backgrounds and political outlook, as well as training experience in joint operations, links between individual terrorists and terrorist groups have increased significantly.[16] Secretive, manipulative, and deceitful recruitment has been quite common among some terrorist groups.[17] They often tend to recruit potential terrorists, usually through known persons and change recruitment strategies by diversifying genders, age groups, and other qualifications. It seems that their bottom-line criterion for the suitability of a terrorist candidate is whatever fits in their needs or those who would endorse their activities.

Training given for terrorist missions is primarily based in or near conflict zones, though some other locations have been used to pre-screen the potential recruits. Ad hoc training over longer periods of time may consist of organized physical exercise designed to establish an *esprit de corps* and basic exposure to operating within a disciplined group environment under a leadership figure—all against the backdrop of extreme ideological learning.

Degree of Disregard to Civilian Injuries

Terrorism is an organized and systematic campaign aimed at inflicting the greatest amount of damage on a civilian population or infrastructure in order to coerce a government to agree to the terrorists' demands. Some even require that the terrorist targets be non-combatants. However, targets may shift to assassinating specific political figure or group. Ultimately, terrorism constitutes a form of psychological warfare directed against a broad civilian audiences.[18] In a well-written essay, it is demonstrated that the term terrorism has been used historically for targeting civilians as a method of affecting political behaviors in nations even though targeting civilians for achieving political goals has failed in the past and it will fail again.[19] In conventional warfare between two countries, military forces generally avoid killing civilian population, and objectives are chosen or victory is decided based on skills, tactics, and weaponry. War between uniformed combatants is generally not considered terrorism. War between nation-states generally aims at destroying the war-making abilities of enemy nations, as well as destroying the armies. As such, though populated areas are targeted, they are usually targeted for their factories and production abilities rather than to kill civilians.[20] The military ethics dictate that civilian population should not, intentionally or unintentionally, be terrorized by military attacks. On the other hand, terrorists often do not distinguish between military and civilian targets and cause injury to civilians, rarely showing regrets for that. To a terrorist, a civilian victim may just be an instrument for the message of attention getter through media and nothing more.[21]

TYPES OF TERRORISM

Several examples of types of terrorism are listed in Table 3.1. I am providing brief comments on these stated below.

Regionally Centered Terrorism. Several terrorist activities have stayed focused only in selected regions of the world. That type of containment is advantageous in dealing with events as well as groups involved with them more effectively than if they were diffused all over the planet.

International/Global Terrorism. As I have pointed out elsewhere, violent religious dissidents have arisen in reaction to modernization and globalization. In addition, some of the terrorist groups have stationed their activities in different parts of the globe hoping to stay active even if they become dislocated or lose their leadership in certain other areas.

Focused on Separatist Groups. Separatism tendencies have political as well as economic dimensions. They have always existed in most areas of the world. Many of them are communalistic and religious groups looking for an identity and a search for independence from a country or a region.[22]

Religious Terrorism. As we will discuss in Chapter 6, this type of terrorism has been gaining strength during the past few decades.

Retributional Terrorists. Retribution as a trend in terrorist activities has been gaining ground during the past several years. It has overlapped with separatism and religious based violence.[23]

Ethno-Nationalist Terrorism. This has been based on racism, ethnicity, language, and related criteria.

Left- and Right-Wing Ideologies. Ranging from ultra-liberal to ultra-conservative ideologies, groups following extremist attitudes in religious, political, and other preferences seek means of violence to prevail.[24]

Anarchist Terrorism. This type of violence has existed for creating chaos and normlessness during the history of mankind.

State-sponsored Terrorism. Various countries have supported terrorism as a measure to counter or control terrorist movements and insurgency. Some of these have been covert. Other cases involve a direct involvement of governments leading terrorist activities.

Demonstrative Terrorism. This type of terrorism has been a sort of political theatre to get publicity.

Narco Terrorism. Many terrorist groups have used narcotics and illegal drugs as a source of supporting violence.

Cyber Terrorism. This form of terrorism is emerging and is likely to become quite effective as it can affect massive numbers of people through the use of technology.

Mass Destruction Terrorism. This appears to be a quantum leap in reference to increasing fear of extensive destruction in the world through powerful means. As a threat, it has potentials of creating impact on large population.

CONCLUDING REMARKS

The chapter provided an overview of the meaning, characteristics, and types of terrorism as a process in contemporary society. Additional illustrations on the process will be given in the next chapter focused on terrorcide. The two chapters will provide a background for explaining and preventing the serious forms of violence.

4

Pathology of Terrorcide

That one virtually destroys himself if he so far abandons his loyalty to reality as to yield to impulses contrary to natural laws or social standards are perhaps obvious. If such a departure is extreme, if the impulses are so powerful as to escape all inhibition and express himself in a chaotic, disorganized fashion without regard to any reality, we have what is designated medically as psychosis and legally as insanity.

—Karl A. Menninger, *Man Against Himself*

What leads people voluntarily to adopt an identity that must end in self-destruction/ none of us is born that way. Suicide attackers are made, not born. How are they made? Why should someone give up the life-loving dreams for which we are selected and prefer an identity that requires detachment from humanity and can only be sustained by a terrible death?

—Mark Harrison,
An Economist Looks at Suicide Terrorism

Suicide bombing is the crack cocaine of warfare. It doesn't just inflict death and terror on its victims; it intoxicates the people who sponsor it.

—David Brooks, *The Culture of Martyrdom*

INTRODUCTION

I chose the word 'terrorcide' in place of 'suicide terrorism' based on a tradition in literature such as the use of a phrase 'autocide' (generally meaning as the use of an automobile to kill oneself). By terrorcide, I imply the use of terrorizing people as one of the assumed reasons for committing suicide. My rationale to use one word rather than two is brevity.

The phenomenon of terrorism has, particularly during the past few decades, added a unique and probably one of the most dangerous styles of violence against the humanity in the form of terrorcide. Individuals engaged in this form of killing are 'true believers'[1] whose only reality is a blind faith in their 'just cause', often legitimized in an apparent sense of desperation without the use of scientific logic for vested interests of their own collective body or group beyond which nothing seem to matter. They generally tend to lose sight of own personal meaning of life and become seriously committed to conversion of the world into their fantasies by turning into the so-called human bombs. Studies have reported an increasing trend in suicide missions for achieving terrorist goals.[2]

Incidents of suicide missions are on the rise in various parts of the world despite of desperate efforts to detect them even in very contained locations.[3] It seems that we currently lack theoretical and methodological capability in almost all disciplines to be able to adequately understand or comprehend all dimensions of this complex process of violence in human society. I do, however, find in the literature numerous anecdotal and historical narratives of incidents and political movements involving suicide terrorists. I particularly find all sorts of interpretations and some time even emotionally charged articles on the subject on the web and in other popular media, often focusing on particular political and 'religious' groups propagating justifications suicide terrorists have. Many of these analyses perhaps distort facts and usually provide limited knowledge of multiple causes and correlates of suicide terrorism and its impacts on lives of people across the globe. Available data on suicide terrorists are often sketchy, sensationalized, or classified under the jurisdiction of various countries. We need systematic research in natural and social sciences for effectively investigating forms and correlates of suicide terrorism in order to deal with this serious problem. I find the sociological perspective as a meaningful approach to study and interpret issues related to the problem. It is a broader perspective that incorporates analyses at various levels (individual, social, cultural, ecological, and so forth).

TYPOLOGY OF TERRORCIDE

Suicide is a pathological process. Being killed is the extreme form of submission just as killing is the extreme form of aggression.[4] It is a murder by self and is a multidimensional malaise. There are multiple contexts and cultural variations of this phenomenon. Factors leading to the problem include biological, psychological, life events, chronic illness, family history, and soc isolation. Suicide is a social process involving the individual's adjustment to death and dying and is related to violence.[5]

Terrorcide has become a leading form of terrorism in the world. It consists of an operational method of terrorism in which the very act of attack is dependent upon the death of the perpetrator. It seems that the attacker is aware that if he/she does not commit self murder, the planned attack will not be implemented. The attack is usually carried out by activating explosives worn or carried on person by the terrorist or planted in a vehicle driven to the planned destination. It is a human missile. The years since 2004 have witnessed a substantial growth in a number of suicide attacks, nearly 500 per cent more than all the years from 1980 to 2003 combined. What started out as a tiny number of terrorcide attacks around the world was climbing at an alarming rate, from an average of three suicide attacks per year in the 1980s to 10 per year in the 1990s to 50 per year from 2000 to 2003 and to 300 per year from 2004 to 2009.[6]

It appears that the problem of terrorism has added newer and more dangerous forms of violence against people through the tactics called terrorcide. It may be carefully planned use of religion for recruiting and training terrorists.[7] Terrorcide is "like lung cancer".[8] It merits special attention because it is a type of terrorism that is responsible for more deaths than any other form of phenomenon. From 1980 to 2002, over 70 per cent of all deaths due to terrorism were the result of terrorcide even though this tactic amounted to only 3 per cent of terrorist attacks. Terrorciders are superpredators. They murder vast numbers of innocent people in each attack. The literature on terrorcide has been flooded with interpretations, strategies for what we need to be doing to counter the movement, stopping the trend, or whatever. It is a complex phenomenon. While scholars as well as practitioners are using adjectives, labels, and ideas on profiling who are these terrorciders and what can be done for preventing/reversing the trend, suicide incidents are increasingly been reported in the news every other day.[9]

Using the Delphi procedures which were described in Chapter 1, I constructed a typology of terrorcide. I believe that after testing the typology through additional empirical testing it may become a contribution to the existing literature. I am proposing only two types of terrorcide, namely (1) collectivistic terrorcide and (2) pathological terrorcide. Each of them has two sub-types. They are discussed below.

1. Collectivistic Terrorcide

It was Durkheim who considered the problem of suicide connected to the collectivity in terms of the degree of social solidarity.[10] I contend that suicide as a self-murder though is related to influences from social collectivity as well as a possibility it is being rationalized the person by blaming society. I will clarify this point in my following discussion.

Pseudo Collectivistic Terrorcide

I have a problem with Durkheim's typology of altruistic suicide, particularly when I try to relate it with terrorcide. Regardless of the intent, the concept of altruism implies elements of sacrifice and selflessness. However, committing suicide for intentionally hurting or killing innocent children, men and women and then saying he sacrificed for community or his group or religion may not be justified to be 'altruistic' as such. The way terrorciders are trained to kill is nowhere close to any form of altruism. A terrorcider is actually a selfish and cruel person regardless of rationalizations. I call it as 'pseudo' altruism instead.

Fanatical Collectivistic Terrorcide

Other form of collectivity orientation applies to fanatic terrorists who have a false consciousness of asceticism and martyrdom in the form of neurotic invalidism characterized by a compulsion to get into pitiable situations and derive comfort from the sympathy aroused by this spotlight. In martyrdom, the individual thinks himself or portrays himself as a hero because of an understanding of scarifying life to the collectivity. Such fanatics actually are 'rational idealists' and fantasize for rewards for sacrificing own life through terrorcide.[11] This appears to be a false and dangerous sense of heroism and assumed altruism. For example, questions have been raised in the literature whether the kamikaze pilots who died crashing into American ships 'bravely' chose or were forced to do so. Are terrorciders made or are born that way? Are they 'volunteers' or programmed like robots? Altruistic suicide results from insufficient individuation and is characterized by energy or activity rather than a motivation for terrorcide as they advocate existence beyond mortal life.[12]

2. Pathological Terrorcide

Psychologically Pathological Terrorcide

Instinct for life is the most important instinct surpassing all other instincts and drives. When a person loses that instinct, he/she is likely to be in some state of psychological abnormality. Suicide is likely to be an escape from an intolerable situation but is self-destruction, is a flight from reality and is seductive because of its simplicity. Killing the innocent is not altruism as people who engage in such behavior may not have self respect but may get 'thrills' from social recognition. They feel power as have no value of own life.[13] Rationality related to violence through suicide is questioned as mental disease.[14] Clinical research has shown that there is a close association between mental disorder and suicidal behaviors. It is more cowardice than heroism.[15] It may be related to suicide risk factors such as depression, delusional depression, schizophrenia, dumbfounded death instinct panic disorder, alcohol abuse, impulsivity, history of family violence, suspiciousness, rebelliousness, loneliness, cocaine abuse, bipolar disorder, and borderline personality disorder.[16]

Socially Pathological Terrorcide

Sociologists consider terrorist suicide bombing is, so to say, the violence of the meek wanting attention.[17] Some even use the "Zealots, the thugs" labels as motivations terrorciders have relate to deviant behavior.[18] It seems that terrorciders are social misfits, desperate for taking revenge. The notion of anomic suicide[19] implying normlessness orientation on part of those committing suicide seems to apply to terrorciders.

EFFECTIVENESS OF TERRORCIDE

Mission Focused

Terrorcide is an effectively planned form of deadly violence requiring a strong commitment to the mission. It is carefully organized activity effectively controlled by the leadership involved. It is not a casual or individualized effort. Its results, consisting of successfully launched attacks, may be hard to understand without realizing that self-sacrifice in the interest of a broader social cause. It is an attack to terrorize and purposefully create fear and panic in the unprepared maximum numbers among the enemy. Its outlook is more people get killed, the better; more damage to property and enemy, the better; and more the media attention and publicity causing a blow to public morale, the better. Democratic countries are generally the major targets of terrorcide attacks as they seem to be uniquely vulnerable to comply with the attackers' wishes.

Hard to Detect

Terrorcide is a surprise attack, secretly planned and enforced. The profiles of those committing suicide attacks keep changing in a cleverly innovative way. For example, it used to have relatively young males as attackers. For the past several years, the organizers have been recruiting young and older females and people wearing religious and police uniforms to gain success in suicide missions.[20] It is meant to be a relatively easy and quickly enforced process in order to make sure that security forces are unprepared and unsuspecting. Since the perpetrator is killed during the course of the attack, so there is no fear of him be caught alive and be interrogated by the security forces endangering future attacks. In addition, these attacks do not require an escape plan as the attacker is planned to be killed. It is therefore extremely difficult to respond to it as it is very unpredictable as to when, where, how it takes place.

Hard to Prevent

Terrorcide attacks are aimed at coercing opponents carrying out their missions in crowded and changing locations in innovative ways. The suicide attack focuses on time and place of target assuring a degree of success. The world is no longer threatened by the great wars. But acts of terrorism by small bands of individuals lurk as an imminent danger, often more ominous and potentially catastrophic than the military forces of earlier times.[21] Becoming a terrorcider is a different process than it used to be in other forms of terrorism. They use newer methods and technology in various attacks, making it difficult to predict their operations.

Cost Effective

Terrorcide operations are relatively cheap. The only cost is life of bomber who wants to die, volunteering in the name of faith. The cost of recruitment and training of attackers is minimal.[22] On the other hand, the impact of the terrorcide missions is grave. So the cost benefit ratio is in favor of the terrorists. In fact, these missions make greater impact than other types of bombing through conventional methods. It is almost impossible to deter a suicide bombing that produces a significant psychological effect on enemy and general public.[23]

Deadliest

Usually, a terrorcider is a relatively simple but a 'smart bomb'. The terrorciders can position themselves in the ideal spot and blow themselves up with precision timing to cause maximum damage. Studies have found that sui bombings have an average of seven to eight times the number of victims as other operational techniques such as shootings or the use of bombs detonated by a timer or by remote control. The planning of suicide attacks is also simple and easy. In addition, they are acts of desperation using and metaphysical goals. They do not show off but are very deadly and chaotic.[24]

Global Impact

Terrorcide is no longer considered a localized or restricted activity. Its scope now is worldwide. An important study assessing the record of suicide missions has concluded that their effectiveness is increasing in multiple parts of the globe and the preventing strategies for their containment are not working out as well.[25]

However, I have an encouraging note despite of statistics on suicide missions. It seems from various sources of information on terrorism, especially from certain parts of the world, that terrorist missions have not made as widespread impact as some studies assessed earlier. During the past several years, except in a rare event,[26] a large number of suicide attacks resulted in fewer deaths and property damage as compared to what may have been expected by organizations planning them. It is estimated that the terrorcide movements has failed to make significant impact in much of the world population because many be people and organizations have not largely been impressed by its logic and strategies. Recent damage done to one major group[27] has caused a set back to terrorcide movement and it is likely that its future may be contained to a limited impact.

CONCLUDING REMARKS

Terrorcide is a serious issue and needs to be researched in the future assessing trends and impacts. It cannot be taken lightly because of its relationship with fanaticism in the religious thought. I will be examining the explanation relevant to this issue in next two chapters and its prevention in Chapters 7 and 8.

5

Toward Explaining Terrorism

Holding on to anger, like grasping a hot coal with the intent of throwing at someone else; you are the one getting burned.

—Gautama Buddha

While there is no scarcity of scientific data on historical accounts of terrorist activities or incidents, many of those seem not to have been put through a conceptual analysis and discussion of explanation and consequences based on critical thinking. I am making a limited effort toward that end.

SELECTED EXPLANATIONS

Psychological Explanation

The goal of psychology as a social science is to understand and predict terrorist behavior. Efforts in that direction demonstrate how and why terrorist attackers think and behave the way they do. I briefly mentioned psychoanalytical approach in reference to terrorcide. Some cognitive theorists, however, have broadened the scope of predicting terrorist behavior by illustrating how suicide tendencies may be better understood by developing an insight on the individual terrorist's thoughts.[1] Other theorists also became disillusioned with the psychoanalytical approach in particular reference to a rather restricted explanation of terrorist behaviors and started to explore the individual terrorist personality and attitudes in a broader context.[2] Some started to understand why the 'terrorist mind' works in the direction of anger and hate.[3] For example, terrorist mind operating from terror to triumph and resilience goes through a complex process and a generally held perception that suicide attackers are deranged fanatics is false; most terrorist operatives are psychologically normal and their attacks are virtually always premeditated.[4] Personal notoriety, anger, revenge, retribution against a perceived injustices, and taking vengeance for their loved one's violent death may not always be psychotic behaviors as such. For example, a widow may perceive death to be better than a life of hopelessness, despair, and disgust. It may not be psychologically 'abnormal' for certain children who grow up in an environment of loved ones' dying and being humiliated hopelessly, and, therefore, may be subtly indoctrinated in a culture glorifying ultimate sacrifice. I am making a point that modern psychologists are trying to conduct more in-depth analysis of terrorist phenomena than done previously.

SOCIOLOGICAL INTERPRETATION

Functionalism

Functionalism articulates ways of strengthening a social system through integration of parts instead of any toleration of deviance and violence that actually paralyze the system. The functionalists conducting research on terrorism recently, however, are taking a broader look at violence in human society as compared to classical theorists such as Durkheim and Parsons. While contemporary theorists still examine or try to understand the suicidal person a soc context where it occurs, they are going into multiple levels of analysis to identify interacting correlates of the problem. Some examine and interpret ideas and data on terrorism through an eclectic application of several sociological interpretations even within the outlook of functionalism paradigm.[5]

While there is no scarcity of scientific data on historical accounts of terrorist activities or incidents, many of those seem not to have been put through a conceptual analysis and discussion based on critical thinking. For example, Durkheim's analysis of 'altruistic suicide' has been re-interpreted by some as relevant to suicide terrorism.[6] Functionalism articulates ways of strengthening a social system through integration of parts instead of any toleration of deviance and violence that actually paralyzes the system. Functionalist studies[7] recognize that the role of religion or altruism has to be carefully interpreted in light of factors such as the degree of religious fanaticism caused by certain political factors and other aspects of social integration operating in particular religious groups or situations. Organizations executing attacks, acquiring weaponry, choosing operatives, targeting victims are all part of social systems.

The Conflict Perspective

The conflict theory paradigm, on the other hand, recognizes the reality of violence in society based on inequality and injustice. However, that paradigm does not necessarily supports extremism nor argues in favor of the violence of hate.[8] Conflict theory, just like other approaches, has variations of outlook some of which tend to inflate conflict while others advocate ways to manage it.[9] One of the major concerns of the conflict theory has been an increasing rate of poverty around the globe despite of economic growth in some countries. Poverty rates in some of those countries are still going up because of population growth there. Poverty now seems to be more serious universal problem than what it was during the last century, particularly because of the increasing issue of 'relative deprivation' among people due to global awareness through mass media. People all over the world now compare their plight with the affluence in some parts of the world. That generates frustration and hostility among people. Problems generated by poverty, therefore, do have impact on the rise of violence and terror. In addition, the rate of immigration and emigration among nations has been increasing. That mobility further creates conflicts and strife among people. However, some sociologists do not consider rising poverty as an important explanation of terrorism.[10] I still think that extreme inequalities across the globe are creating stress and may at least partially explain recruitment of some of the terrorists.

Studies indicate that reported acts of violence against impoverished women in interpersonal relationships are generally higher than those in middle and upper classes. Research reports have consistently demonstrated that women in low income families, including single mothers and minority groups, are at a higher risk of being physically, sexually, and emotionally abused by men in relationships and social encounters. A majority of prostitutes in the third-world countries are found to have come from financially helpless background. Poverty-stricken women are not found to be autonomous and self-confident, thereby becoming readily accessible to patriarchal controls or dominance as compared to those who are educated and financially self-sufficient. These women are likely to stay as victims in violent relationships several times longer than those in other social classes. They tend to become a part of the so-called 'cycle of violence' by passing on their victimization and helplessness from one generation to the other. I addition, children who grow in impoverished environments are also likely to become victims of neglect, abandonment, sexual molestation, physical beating, psychological or emotional abuse, underpaid labor, harassment by peers in school, and other multiple forms of exploitation. Growing up in those environments promotes juvenile delinquency, early-age substance abuse, gangs, high rates of school dropouts, and unhealthy lifestyles.

Exchange Behaviorism

Behaviorist exchange theory advocates an approach of reciprocity based on rational and pragmatic reasoning in societal relationships. Behaviorist exchange theory advocates an approach of reciprocity based on rational and pragmatic reasoning in societal relationships.[11] Explaining violence from this perspective, terrorists are goal focused and launch or participate in campaigns of attacks carried out through well organized groups for specific political motives. In cost/benefit terms, terrorist attacks are financially attractive as there are often attractive monetary rewards for attackers and their families along with 'honor' and sympathy from community members as intrinsic rewards.[12]

Consisting of three-steps campaign stated below, terrorist attacks usually attract more publicity and honor than other types of attacks:

1. A strategic logic of terrorism providing useful political purpose; terrorists would not have gone for it by coercion or a lack of rewards;

2. There has to be some degree of societal support such as community's glorification and martyrdom; and

3. There has to be some logic based on faith in certain attractive benefits for him/her choose the option of violence (sometime, an individual makes preparations getting ready for the ultimate step, often, making sure that he/she has explosives or a cyanide capsule to commit suicide if the mission failed).[13]

From the rationality based exchange theory perspective, we can talk about some facilitators of terrorism. Two of them are briefly stated below. The notion of 'facilitator' is different from complex analyses of cause-effect relations or even correlates of a phenomenon. It mainly identifies factors that may help the terrorist activity in terms of such as underlying motives and meanings assumed to be relevant.

Facilitator 1: Political Independence and Separatism. There are separatist movements going on various parts of the world. They, in relationship with supporting groups and harboring nations, become involved in independence oriented movements in search of a separate identity from a country or a larger group. Separatism intends divisiveness based on factors such as ethnicity, religion, territorial identity line, and so forth.[14] Reports on such movements often accuse particular leaders, often perceived to be charismatic who may have specific interest in separating from a country or region.

Facilitator 2: Role of Mass Media. Mass media, including internet and cell phones, facilitated by satellites have created revolution in our so-called 'communication-information' age. We know that every change, including current developments in technology, has cost-benefit ratio. Not that we are going to want to go back to the dark ages of ignorance, we may still

want to understand how information technology may not only
be used for the 'right' reasons but could also have potentials of
being abused or used for the 'wrong' reasons.[15] It is contented
that the mass media helps the terrorism process. Terrorism that
relies upon the media to spread the terrorists' cause will choose
a target in order to attract this mass attention.[16] Afterwards, as
the terrorists hope, the mass media descends, the group and its
talking points are referenced, and the terrorists consider this a
victory. Propaganda abuse of media is a known reality. I tell
my students in classes that the internet has a lot of 'good'
information but also has some 'garbage' sensational stuff as
well. The challenge for us is to be smart and critical thinker
about what we choose to read and believe. For example, media
openly give information on how to make a bomb, who the
'martyrs' and what choice someone may have in finding miss
or mister perfect for marriage. We just have to watch out! I do
not advocate any censorship.[17] However, we may want to
advocate being somewhat responsible in avoiding feeding into
confusion, fears, and opinions that may create perceptions that
is not meant by the media organizations.

IDENTIFYING A PROFILE OF TERRORISTS

I am making a limited attempt to profiling terrorists based
on the Delphi methodology outlined in Chapter 1. The major
objective is to use the sociological perspective toward
identifying selected characteristics of terrorists. My specific
objectives include the development of ideas for outlining a
tentative profile of suicide and other terrorists as an intellectual
exercise in attempting to build a tentative and general profile.
In doing so, I did not attempt to target any particular nation,
ethnic, religious, separatist or political groups as such.

A few studies have demonstrated that profiling is emerging
as a "legitimate adjunct" to criminal investigation.[18] The
Delphi procedures facilitated the final selection and ranking
of psychological, demographic/economic, and sociopolitical
characteristics of people who were considered to be engaging
in acts of terrorism around the globe on the basis of consensus
among professionals and community leaders as experts.
Selected characteristics of terrorists are outlined below.

Personality Profiles of Terrorists

- Emotionally charged for militancy against particular govt./authority;
- dependent, particularly on some specific person(s) of authority;
- have inferiority/superiority complex;
- believe that violence is the only way to defend self, family, community, or nation from the perceived aggressions by others;
- low self-esteem but a false/irrational sense of courage/confidence;
- a lack of specific goals and direction;
- sense of desperation; depression;
- sense of having experienced significant loss/deprivation;
- pessimistic;
- nomadic (unsettled) lifestyle;
- loner and egocentric;
- obsessive/compulsive;
- anxiety disorder;
- serious temper/anger control problems;
- rash/erratic;
- authoritarian and controlling;
- focused on blaming someone/something particular or general for own problems;
- inflexible/rigid, resisting change and having perseverance in perusing same cause and behaviors over time;
- experienced a dramatic change in the recent past;
- tend to label people/nations without giving a second thought;
- individuals having a history of a certain degree of mental illness, emotional disturbance or psychopathology;

- a history of overt/covert suicidal tendencies;
- hysteric;
- manipulative;
- phobic/hateful of law enforcement and military people;
- substance abuser;
- single-minded;
- recruited at young age; and
- fatalistic.

Demographic Characteristics of Terrorists

- Largely young, single, males recruited at tender age;
- none or unstable employment history;
- relatively lower socio-economic status, including low or a conditioned/highly regulated/programmed schooling;
- a low rate of inter-generational/intra-generational mobility;
- do not advocate population control; and
- likely to belong to particular ethnic or religious background.

Socio-political Background of Terrorists

- Fanatic and radical interpretation of a religion;
- having expectation or received viable publicity for a cause through media;
- a vocal lack of trust in legal recourses such as negotiations/collaborations/conflict resolutions and in organizations that provide help in those internationally;
- having been over-socialized and controlled from childhood;
- obsessive belief in familism or kinship;
- obsession in a separatist political ideology;

- tend to be over committed to a particular cause/movement;
- dictatorial political activism;
- family/affiliated-group history of violence;
- having been a victim of violence or abuse, or had a family member/friend who has been a victim of violence and terror;
- recipient of financial and emotional support from a terrorist group/individual(s);
- having an access to a training facility for terrorism;
- usage of schools to train/recruit future terrorists;
- ethnocentric and has a racial/religious prejudicial orientation toward select groups;
- having own or close family or friends' criminal and/or suicide history;
- want publicity from media through whatever means possible;
- have no commitment to social order;
- anomic; and
- uses foreign powers as scapegoats.

CONSEQUENCES OF TERRORISM

It seems that terrorism as a form of violence does not accomplish anything positive in human society. Perhaps even the institutional wars have occasionally produced social and economic reforms and advancements. It is not that I justify human warfare; it does seem that at least few times in human history wars were based on serious goals. However, I am not sure if most terrorists have or lead to the accomplishment of any goals per se. Are they destructive enthusiasts as such? Do they merely act in vain? Do they even realize the seriousness of their acts? Of course, they do produce consequences. I hope to identify selected examples of some of them in a table in this chapter implying from a general impact to ones relation to specific terrorist events.[19] Impacts of terrorist acts on society and people have been noted in the literature in number of ways, ranging from severe trauma to victims to indirect effects. One of the major impacts concerns the so-termed 'contagion effects' implying consequences that have chain reactions of consequences affecting a large number of people and the environment in significant ways directly or indirectly. The impact of terrorism on human society has been in that mode. It has affected direct victims injured or killed, included even bystanders horrified. Physical impacts, for example, have included changes in body chemistry and on brain leading to multiple problems.[20]

I have enumerated a number of consequences through an empirical investigation based on the Delphi procedures. These are listed in Table 5.1. As indicated in the table, terrorists make multiple impacts in various areas of society in the short as well as long run. While it is difficult to assess all consequences of their actions, some studies have been completed assessing psychological, political, economic, and social impacts assessing whatever damage they may have caused. Some studies do mention profound and unproductive or destructive consequences effect of terrorist phenomenon.[21]

At the individual level, victims of terrorist attacks have been particularly impacted in significant ways. Some got traumatized by going through the experience of violence. That affected their ability to cope with stress in the long run. It is difficult, of course, to assess emotional or psychological injuries people experience by going through fear and the post traumatic stress disorders.[22] In addition, terrorism disrupts normal family and community living. In particular, people living in regions where terrorist activities are intense have a highly insecure life. Exposure to significant level of violence negatively affects quality of life, including the morale of people. Studies have, for example, indicated affect on freedom and privacy of citizens in a country after experiencing an important terrorist event.[23] For example, the fear of terrorism has spawned a massive security industry aimed at protecting individuals, tourists, travelers, institutions and industries.[24] In addition, at the economic and political level, terrorism has resulted in destabilizing economies and governments. Perhaps, it is one of the most important agents of negative changes in various areas of our lives that are so difficult to assess.[25]

Table 5.1: Examples of Selected Impacts of Terrorism Based on Sociological Research

Types of Impact	Short-Term Impact	Long-Term Impact
Individual/ Psychological	• Panic, shock, confusion • Anxiety, fear and anger • Post traumatic stress disorder • Victimization	• Mental illness • Drug addiction • Suicide rates rise • Sense of insecurity rises • Alienation and apathy
Political/Economy	• State sponsored terrorism increase • Stepped up security measures • Disruption in govt. functioning • Volatility and imbalance in the economy • Political instability • Disruption in the economy	• Instability in Government • Expansion of state regulations and interventions • Reduction in individual freedom and privacy • Rise in poverty rate and unemployment • Rise in emigration and immigration at global level
Sociocultural	• Increase in socio-emotional cohesion/solidarity • Disruption in social order • Increase in crime rates, including hate crimes • Refugees increase • Destabilization of social institutions • Communities dislocated	• Contagion effects • Anomie: Increase in crime rate, family violence, suicides & divorce rates • Violence as a way of life • Lack trust and low morale in social order • Interpersonal stress • Lack of social cohesion • Increase in diversity, divisiveness, social conflicts

CONCLUDING REMARKS

I realize that my effort to profile suicide terrorists may be considered by some to be rather tentative. I also do not know whether my listing of characteristics and behaviors of such terrorists is literally comprehensive, inclusive of all major dimensions of terrorism, reliable and valid. Scientific data on profiles of suicide terrorists are not openly available in the literature, except in selected books and articles that talk about unique historical and individual characteristics of certain terrorist groups or persons. It is difficult to check on the validity of our list by comparing it with specific terrorist individual or group. I do, however, feel a sense of accomplishment in being able to develop an initial profile of suicide terrorists with the help of literature as well as of seemingly interested university teachers, researchers, and community leaders who spent considerable amount of time in selecting, ranking and grouping profile characteristics through common sense, conceptual thought and rational logic. I am confident that the Delphi procedures enabled me meaningfully to becoming better organized and systematic in developing the profile.

The chapter outlines some ideas on explaining and assessing terrorism. The next chapter focuses on the role of religious explaining terrorist activities. These assessments should aid in outlining some preventive steps to overcoming and adjusting to the phenomenon of terrorism.

6

Rationalization for Using Religion

Sectarianism, bigotry, and it's horrible descendant fanaticism, have long possessed this beautiful earth. They filled the earth with violence, drenched it often with human blood, destroyed civilization, and sent whole nations to despair...I fervently hope that the bell that tolled this morning in honor of this convention may be the death knell of all fanaticism....

—Swami Vivekananda at the
World Parliament of Religions on the
opening day in
Chicago on September 11, 1893

Logic has never been the strong point of any established religion. Nor has there been room for accommodation of a different point of view in the minds of religious bigots.

—Khushwant Singh

It may be that religion is dead, we had better known it and set ourselves to try to discover other sources of moral strength before it is too late.

—Pearl S. Buck

INTRODUCTION

Terrorists and terrorist organizations, including governments in a few countries, have taken an increased interest during the past few decades in articulating religious reasoning to rationalize or justify violent means for achieving their political and economic goals.[1] However, no formal religion in the world seems to be actually condoning violence against innocent people. Often, it is some zealots and terrorist leaders, who add varying interpretations to beliefs and rituals for meeting particular needs of believers.[2] I contend that if the institution of religion has been misused by some, it is time that we reverse the cycle and recognize its "right or proper" use in human relationships, probably by rejecting initiatives adopted by some for employing religious beliefs or ideas for condoning violence in any form. As implied in my last three chapters, contemporary societies need to develop and adopt an optimistic tone that seeks to find the future-oriented ways of preventing religion-based violence against the humanity and enhance the opportunities for either leaving religion alone or using it to promote a global peace instead.

It seems that many scholars and political leaders in the past considered religion to be the antithesis of violence. The fact that religion is so frequently involved in communal violence for the past few decades raises intriguing questions about faith, religious organizations, and religious leaders.[3] Most of the so-termed 'great' or 'established' world religions through their scriptures and formal teachings are known for forgiveness, kindness, harmony, and peace, generally staying away from political ideologies and conflicts despite some incidents of over-zealots now and then. Spiritual matters have often taken stand against causing injuries to innocent men, women and children through compassionate and divine outlooks. Why now are several of the religious groups talking about 'holy wars' and other pretence dividing the humanity on the planet? Is that a religious outlook or is religion being 'used or abused' for political and economic causes? It is plausible that the institution of religion does not directly advocate violence against the humanity and generally recognizes a need for protecting innocent civilians. However, there is some evidence that religious violence is among the most pressing, unreasonable, and dangerous issues facing the world community today.[4]

MEANING AND ORIGIN OF RELIGION

It seems almost impossible to define religion, even though numerous scholars and religious thinkers have attempted to comprehend its components and varied interpretations of its stated and implied meanings in multiple contexts. I do not plan to indulge in all sorts of complexity of the phenomenon of religion in human society, except at least hint on some of its meanings and interpretations particularly meaningful in the context of violence and terrorism.

Overall, religion is an institutionalized set of beliefs and rituals based on metaphysical (implying something or some idea based on a faith that is 'beyond matter, observation, and even logic') sort of a super-empirical reference. Thus, religion goes beyond the phenomenological (or perceived) as well as the so-called 'objective' reality, making efforts toward conceptualizing the ontological level of truth. One could be bewildered and literally lost, almost thinking in vain, by going into logics of 'proof' by putting the religious notions to any form of scientific logic as such. In a way, the degree of 'faith' may differ from one religion to the other and even among people in general, ranging from an unquestioned conviction for religious ideas to their total disbelief.[5]

I also need to clarify a distinction between two inter-connected dimensions of religion as a (i) philosophy or ideology (the belief system is deeper and more meaningful than being an emotional zealot) and (ii) as a social institution. In its former sense, it consists of ideas providing people a particular moral and worthy perspective or a way of approaching and leading life, currently and/or beyond. As an institution, it is a form of organization, consisting of principles, traditions or rules of behaviors, and often a stratified structure of positions responsible for its functioning. While I will briefly talk about both in the following section of the chapter, I will refer more to the institutional aspect of religion while discussing its relationship with violence and terrorism. Of course, as stated in the Preface, I shall not imply any reference to particular religions or religious groups as being the 'divisive forces,'[6] historically or in current societies in any part of the world so that we can talk only in conceptual context here.

Religion is one of the oldest institutions, perhaps as old as families, ethnicities, and nomadic tribes. It also has a history of complexity in terms of diverse forms and styles of belief systems as well as rituals and practices. In fact, the religious thought has generally been fragmented in being plagued by diversity, divisions, and even rankings implied by some groups. There have been elements in multiple religions of co-existence as well as inconsistencies, compatibilities and contradictions, and adjustments as well as conflicts among the world religions and religious groups. To begin with perhaps, there were just simple totems in primitive societies symbolizing their collectivity in some ways and their 'religious' visions and meanings of faith.

Some anthropologists believe that fear of death and other sources of stress in environment led primitive people into beliefs in the magical and religious ways offering hope for such ideas as salvation and immortality. What some people at the time might have sought to seek was either the transitory consolation of momentary oblivion or a miraculous redemption in the afterlife, depending on whatever they did choose to conceptualize.[7] That perhaps led to a beginning of a religious vision for human beings further progressing into limitless dreams and ideologies ending in a complex situation of diversity of related ideas in today's world.

FUNCTIONS OF RELIGION

Religions and religious groups of various sizes and scope have provided human society multiple functions for thousands of years. I am stating below selected examples of functions identified by anthropologists, historians, and social philosophers.

Sense of Security

Philosophical and anthropological studies have logically summarized the history of religious thought providing the individual a sense of dependence, security and hope even while dealing natural disasters, calamities, and various unknown phenomena, including death, at the primitive as well as modern stages of human evolution.[8] As I stated earlier, religion is not restricted by studying 'realities' only through empirical observation, its metaphysical domain helped individuals deal with super-empirical aspects of the world.

Social Integration and Solidarity

Anthropologists and sociologists, such as Malinowski and Durkheim, systematically identified the role of religious beliefs and rituals in producing as sense of social solidarity and cohesion in human society. When people participate in rituals and prayers collectively, they develop a sense of identity emotional bondage what was termed by Durkheim as "mechanical solidarity". Religious practices provide members of congregation bondage and orientations around the common goals set in their belief system.

Religion and Psychological Well-being

The idea that religion has something to do with psychological well-being and mental health of the individual is hardly new. A classical study on sick and healthy mindedness[9] and on the role of religion in contributing to personal growth and maturity[10] are well known. Other empirical studies have identified how religion provides socio-emotional support in dealing with mental and physical illness.[11] In addition, research has established the importance of religious faith in medical healing and recovery.[12] Religious convictions help the individual in adjusting to death and dying process as well.[13] Religion is considered as a significant source of comfort and peace of mind to the individual during periods of stress, depression, and suicidal tendencies.[14] Religion provides an escape from hedonistic and materialistic desires and takes the individual toward another level of simplicity and contentment.[15]

Moral Values and Social Control

Sociologists, particularly functionalists, consider the institution of religion as one of the most important sources of social control and order in human society. All major religions divulge into what is right and what is wrong, becoming contributors to moral and traditional values that have played role in the development of laws and justice systems as human beings started to become civilized.[16] Religions have symbolized to some extent the 'power' of society. It has the availability of sanctions and punishments for 'sins' available through notions such as heaven and hell. Some of the religious sanctions have been important for producing conformity to social order among the masses. In addition, religion has provided significant support to the functioning of primary social institutions such as marriage and family.

Religion and Progress

Max Weber has been one of the leading sociologists who questioned the validity of Karl Marx's assumption of religion as opium for the masses has produced 'false consciousness' among the masses leading to their exploitation.[17] Instead, he demonstrated how change in religious ideology such as the protestant ethics led to the development of the 'spirit of capitalism' in the modern economy. That change in the economy has opened new directions for economic progress.[18]

DEGREE OF RELIGIOSITY

There have always been people and communities that have not believed in religion. Overall, however, the institution of religion has operated in varying degrees of intensity and impact ranging from a great deal of moderation to serious forms of extremism and radicalism as briefly illustrated below.

Moderate Spirituality

Low to a moderate degree of religious belief and practice ranges from some degree of skepticism and agnosticism to a 'practical' or 'workable' level of religiosity depending on several factors such as those outlined below.[19]

- Age
- Gender
- Family's religious background and socialization

- People's attitudes toward and perceived benefits of religion
- Socio-economic status
- Type and level of educational attainment
- Ethnicity and nationality
- Degree of modernism.

There has been a trend toward some people believing in spirituality but not in religion in the traditional sense.[20] That change is based on how some people have been treating religion being different from 'being religious' or thinking to being religious but deciding not to actively participate in rituals and collective prayers on regular bases. Some others like to keep religion as a private matter and stay away from being titled or labeled by any name or organizational affiliation.

Religious Fanaticism

As shown in Table 6.1, there are different examples of forms and characteristics of tendencies, orientations and behaviors relevant to the so-termed extremism and fanaticism.[21] The fanatic people, particularly those who take this character seriously tend to be always right, have a syndrome of being enthusiast zealot, and tend to have an unbeatable motivation to be faithful to their beliefs. Rationality for the survival of that religion in their thinking is built in and cannot be negotiated for change. People who speak against it are not just critics, but may be called as infidels or manifestations of some devil figure. Emotivism often views religious commitment and conversion as emotional reactions than intellectual knowledge of the belief system. As such, the 'faithful' individuals can look at their political enemies as also their religious enemies, and see them not as simply possessing a different philosophy but possessing a heretical or even demonic philosophy that must be destroyed. This gives some of them a clear sense of purpose as well as an immediate existential threat where, otherwise, neither might actually be present. In this way, the institution of religion is generally used by fanatics to promote terrorism through hateful means.

Table 6.1: Examples of Orientations and Characteristics of Fanaticism under Three Sub-Headings

Fanatic Tendencies	Characteristics of Orientations and Behaviors
Commitment to Fanaticism	• Uncompromising determinism • Egocentric altruism • Fanaticism as a source of power and pride in oneself • Blind following and loyalty through conditioning and brain washing • Psychological dependence on projected fantasy • Being entitled for supremacy and dominance • Vengeful goals of violence and terrorism
Motivation for Fanaticism	• Zealously wanting a 'pure religion' • Militancy is enthusiasm for achieving worthy goals • Religious awakening • Slavery and worship to various rituals/ways, not ideology • Authoritarian restriction on freedom of choice • Intolerant; excessive irrational zeal • Being 'always right' in using coercive and persecuting means for eliminating those who do not 'fit' • Focus and dependence on fantasies and wishful thoughts • Unconstrained and lethal violence against the 'enemy' • Conquest over dissidents
Principles of Fanaticism	• Fanaticism proclaims owning the only truth and its interpretation; the cardinal truth cannot be exaggerated or overstated and needs no proof • Follow fideism or blind belief that has no philosophy • Keep philosophy simple, straight, final, and obscure; tells what to think and not how to think • Radicalism, fundamentalism, and orthodoxy are infallible • Devine beliefs are unquestionable; rational reasoning leads to skepticism and distortion • Deification and survival sanctified • Emotivism or making emotions primary for belief • End justifying means • Only one way for justice and fairness • Only a particular faith can protect and make people secure

Religious Terrorism

I mentioned in the Preface how religion has been connected to terrorism. Religious factors came out to be some of the major causes of terrorism while I was trying to 'explain' that form of violence in Chapter 5. Additional examples of religious terror may include some states based on theocracy in which non-religious populations may be discriminated and harassed. In addition, some of such states are known for supporting terrorism overtly or covertly.[22]

CONCLUDING REMARKS

It appears that all religions, including any cults and organizations based on spiritual matters, should be kept out of political and economic constraints of being judged or ranked. That idea in this chapter does bring out the importance of trying to understand fanaticism that seems to have plagued almost all world religions. I hope we address this issue more and more through systematic research and open debates. While each religion may be of utmost value to its believers, we need to advocate and practice the principles of equality and freedom of religions around the globe. I will address the issues of secularism and non-violence dealing with that in next two chapters.

7

Preventive Strategies for Terrorism

Should we not contemplate with rejoicing a new future for our planet, peaceful at last, sleeping quietly at last after coming to the end of the long nightmare of pain and horror?

—Bertrand Russell

Violence in itself, because it cannot perform the reconciling and compromising function, leads to the suppression rather than resolution of conflict; it drives conflict underground but does little to eliminate it.

—Kenneth Boulding

Congress shall make no law respecting an establishment of religion, or prohibiting the free exercise thereof; or abridging the freedom of speech, or of the press; or the right of the people peaceably to assemble, and to petition the government for a redress of grievances.

—*The First Amendment to the U.S. Constitution*

India's Constitution guarantees the Fundamental Rights of all citizens and prohibits any discrimination on grounds of religion, race, caste, sex or place of birth.

—Jawaharlal Nehru

MEANING OF PREVENTION

Prevention involves predicting, planning, averting, obstructing, and even forestalling destructive forces fixing to disrupt our lives in significant ways. It is based on principles of righteousness, wisdom, and courage for confronting undesirable forces of terrorism from becoming part of established reality on earth. The saying that maintains "prevention is better than the cure" does have an inspirational meaning implying a significant step of identifying and planning stern measures to combat terrorist forces before they overpower us.

The process of prevention involves (i) anticipating a problem to occur, and (ii) developing ideas, strategies and actions for stopping or hindering the problem before it occurs. Preventive actions may help a person or society to get prepared to deal or cope with a problem effectively. It may also reduce the impact of the problem even if it could not be fully stopped.

Preventive thoughts generally create not only courageous but also constructive and healthy outlooks in dealing with challenges of life. Prevention requires planned interventions with the help of ideas and strategies based on systematic research on already existing ideas in the literature along with new ideas based on empirical research, particularly focused on the specific problem we may be trying to prevent. We will need to identify information about where, how and when a problem of violence may occur, what possible risks are, who will be at risk. Then, we disseminate the information to people at risk as well as security agents when possible without delay. Steps must be taken to overcome contagion effects when needed. We also may need to be prepared to arrange help to dealing with possible harm to potential victim, along with helping those who may need assistance for coping with impacts of whatever intensity or extensity. The adaptation to problems and their impacts helps everyone involved reduce stress by being calm and composed through tolerance and courage to face the realities without having panic attacks, nervous breakdown, or whatever additional undesirable consequences after the events have occurred.

PRIORITIZING PREVENTION OF TERRORISM

Value of Prevention

Based on my discussions in Chapter 2 as well as in other chapters, it is obvious that violence has become a glaring reality of contemporary human society. Does that mean we give up on the prospects of peace and a secure life on this planet? Is doom and gloom perspective acceptable to human beings many of whom claim to be the 'most intelligent' of all known species? Is it acceptable to explore some alternatives to a life stricken by anger, hostility, hatred, and despair? A belief in the finality and irreversibility of evil implies a refusal to accept responsibility to act and look for good in human nature to eliminate evil. By focusing occasionally on a sense of doom and gloom,[1] we tend to deteriorate our courage and creativity to resolve the problem through a calm and constructive pragmatism of 'hope' and 'civility.'[2]

By the 19th century, scholars started recognizing the value of each individual and of life. That perspective led to saving people's lives by advocating steps for preventing destructive behaviors based on psychological and social disturbances. Preventing problems through proactive planning is a rational activity and has become a priority in the area of violence across the globe. The so-called 'science of prevention' provides us tools for becoming prepared in meeting challenges of problems likely to occur in the future. It will contribute to the literature used by those trying to reduce the economic and social costs associated with threats and occurrences of violence. We will identify the worldwide implications of our study for making an impact on the societal ability to learn from terrorist incidents along with continuing a struggle for future prevention.

Terrorist occurrences have been on the rise during the past thirty or so years more than ever before in almost every corner of our planet. The potential for as well as incidents of terrorism in today's world have not only increased but have also become relatively more global, often conducted by transnational and non-state actors. These individuals are well-financed, difficult to penetrate, and have increased access to creative technology and all sorts of weapons of destruction.[3] Prevention may help reduce the surprise element in serious forms of violence enabling us to cope and endure consequences at a tolerable level. We particularly need preventing strategies that may have long range impacts rather than ban-aid approaches providing short-term solutions. However, it is disappointing that the United Nations in its 2005 Summit on Peace Building "neglected to establish the responsibility to prevent terrorism".[4] It is important that we go beyond politics of decision-making in world bodies and explicitly advocate and establish public's concern with the ability to predict and prevent violent deaths in the future through timely actions. We need to reaffirm professional interests of sociologists, criminologists, psychologists, and investigators from other fields to prevent deadly violence.[5] Empirical studies are needed that could have implications for legislators, law enforcement agencies, and pro-active leaders by identifying ways of early identification and prevention of possible terroristic threats in the future. Studies need to reflect on how and why terrorist individuals and groups become 'marginalized' and 'isolated' through their unreasonable use of violence.[6]

Barriers to Prevention

Preventing problems before they occur often is not as easy as it sounds. There are many difficulties and obstacles before plans for prevention may be made and implemented. Some of the examples of barriers facing preventive measures are stated below.

First, preventing problems such as terrorism is a serious and complex process. We have to consider identifying the major factors related to or affecting the occurrence of terrorist incidents. That will require timely and systematic research as well as aggressively involved intelligence or investigating agencies to gather information on when, how, and where terrorist incidents are likely to happen. If that research is thorough, we may then have to decide how we can intercept and stop the incidents from happening. Realizing that an interception may or may not be the 'right' one, careful planning and its implementation will have to be required. In addition, all agencies collecting and organizing intelligence information on possible terrorist incidents have to share various pieces of information and coordinate their efforts in order to be effective in implementing preventive measure. However, many agents as well as agencies are often territorial and autonomous about their operations, particularly based in cross-national settings, and may not always coordinate preventive efforts with each other.

Second, terrorism is too complex and fluid phenomenon to prevent. News media make the situation even more complex as multiple stories and interpretations of terrorist events circulate, often causing confusion and ambivalence about what really happened. People with vested interests in the event contribute to either secrecy or circulating misinformation in the media.

Third, there often are people who deny access to information on a terrorist event. Some also refuse to acknowledge the realities of terrorist organizations and plans for political reasons. Some just do not want to be involved. We therefore, have a number of reasons blocking open communication in hostile situations. Some of the reasons may include ignorance, fears of reprisals, guilt, irrationality, and name-calling. For example, naming and labeling separatist and religious groups may become counter-productive in opening international dialogues for prevention.[7] Selfless leadership is often lacking because of complexity of international economic political situations causing delays in developing open and truthful communication on terrorist issues. Terrorist issues are not only complex but they involve sensitive matters related to territoriality or sovereignty, religious and political autonomy, and economic or business interests that may create obstacles for discussing terrorist problems, particularly at the international level.

Fourth, many political leaders prefer to work on short-range remedial solutions and shy away from idealistically conceptualized curative ideologies such as secularism and non-violence. I will be providing additional comments on those later in this chapter and the next one.

Levels of Prevention

Primary Prevention. It is a serious form of prevention and is oriented toward a comprehensive understanding of the terrorism problems in order to develop long-term and curative (not band-aid) programs for prevention. This approach likes to go to the depth of the problem rather than seeking peripheral information on it. It would investigate and address the major sources of the issues involved and seek long-lasting means or resources for attacking the roots of the problem. It would increase awareness of the problem through media, and identify risks and benefits of prevention. It would also be transparent in providing continual evaluation of any program implementation for prevention for accountability purpose.

Secondary/Tertiary Prevention. It is sort of 'something is better than nothing' strategy. It is needed particularly in the short run to investigate a terrorist problem, intervene as much as possible for corrective actions, treat injuries, repair damage caused by violent episode, provide compensation/protection to victims, seek changes in policies for security, consider changing legal ways, increase opportunities for survivors in the future, and reorganize/regroup for future attacks.

STRATEGIES FOR PREVENTING TERRORISM

Literature relevant to violence and terrorism has diverse and valuable information on 'combating, controlling, containing' and preventing terrorism. I have chosen only three categories for summarizing selected examples of prevention. These are listed in Table 7.1 and briefly discussed below.

Managing Global Inequalities

There have been some approaches dealing with the understanding as well as dealing with international issues by treating the world as artificially divided into areas or regions based on economic and racial criteria. For example, one particular has been widely used for the past many years treating certain countries 'core' and 'developed' while others as 'peripheral' and 'developing' and so forth in a way labeling

then arbitrarily despite of proclaimed criteria used.[8] That type
of a divisive approach does not appear to be an effective way

Table 7.1: Examples of Strategies for Preventing the
Spread of Terrorism into the Future of Humanity

Areas of Preventive Strategies	Intervention
Managing Global Inequalities	• Identify ways of developing prospects of achieving a 'one-world' by overcoming hierarchies of multiple 'worlds' based on economic and political inequities. • Globalize and promote equality of opportunities and deliberate rankings of people and groups based on ethnicities, religions, and genders to overcome violence, discrimination, and bigotry in all areas such as education, employment, health care, and community living.
Improving Education and Information	• Overcome ignorance among common people around the world about violent groups who seek divisiveness for seeking selfish and vested interests and power agendas. • Increasing communicative interconnectivity among people in all corners of the world through new technology. • Identify and internationally declare violence as a serious public health issue in all countries. • Develop educational media programs in multiple languages seeking accurate knowledge and public awareness to prevent interpersonal violence through conflict management. • Seek avenues for 'responsible journalism' in mass media to reduce publicity given to terrorist events, and prevent propaganda launched by terrorist groups. • Openly publicize negative impacts of all terrorism. • Encourage balancing protection of economic prosperity and eco-system to sustain a desirable quality of life through controlling overpopulation as well as overconsumption.
Expanding International Avenues for Enhanced Security	• Enhance the scope of international collaborative alliances for protecting all areas of the world from terrorist movements. • Stop the spread of weaponry and terror alliances by initiating new moves through international organizations. • Promote the scope of peace through democracy, secularism, and nonviolent strategies.

global relationships at least in today's world. Newer studies, in ways to recognize unique contributions of all religions of the world regardless of any hierarchies. In fact, we need to create solidarity and oneness in the world to promote ways of dealing and preventing deadly sources of violence.[9] We need to intervene together at the global level to meet with the challenges of serious forms of violence rather than thinking about who is first or second class citizen on this planet. We really have to put together all of our resources to jointly make a differences in ways innocent human beings are being killed for vested interests.[10] We should instead spend our resources in conducting empirical research and developing policies to meet the challenges of preventing horrifying prospects of a collapse of our planet. Ideas are increasingly developing in the literature on how we can and should develop equalities than divisive ways for minimizing inequalities around us in every possible way.

Improving Education and Information

We live in an age of great potentials for education, technology, and information so widely and effectively available. It seems we have the intelligence and resources to inform people and educate them about what is going on in terrorist attacks meaninglessly killing innocent working human beings. There are no excuses for ignorance and misinformation as we have the capability to get it in every possible way. I have listed some strategies in Table 7.1 for addressing the improvements in increasing educational opportunities and openly confront public issues concerning deadly examples of violence. Mass media and interconnectivity among people will be bound to help overcome ignorance and fear that have lately been in abundance. For example, why cannot we hold media for sensationalizing terrorist acts? After all, we keep them in business. An expert on media makes three points: (i) the media are very much a tool of terrorism, (ii) the media are also a sort of fuel for terrorism, and (iii) media can be a weapon against terrorism.[11] Why do not we openly confront leaders of terrorism through our own constructive type of publicity on how greedy and prejudiced individuals are infecting us with bugs of violence?[12] Responsible journalism is needed in this regard so that every form of notoriety is denied to them. It may be accomplished through the self-regulation by the media.

Expanding International Avenues for Enhanced Security

Increased research will be needed at the international level to provide defense against the use of weapons of mass destruction and other forms of aggression against civilian population. Security in today's global society may not become effective if it is provided only to selected few nations or just to some privileged people. It will need to be enforced internationally for all for reducing the risk of terrorism.[13] Strategies will be needed for planning resources and measures to build potentials for security to avoid international threats and proliferation of and preoccupation with terrorist incidents. We will need to create comprehensively based actions (such as closing down financial resources for supporting terrorist groups) rather than piecemeal and underfunded projects to overcome rhetoric of being attacked. We may also prohibit any acts of violence of an international character that would also contain punitive sanctions aimed at countries providing refuge for terrorist offenders.[14] We really need more and more allies for peace to rebuild and heal.[15] International collaborations and efforts will be needed for developing networks for dialog to strengthen peace operations. Scholars are already talking about peace research as a science and peace by peaceful means to overcome structural violence.[16]

SECULARISM AS STRATEGIC PREVENTION

A recent study provides a fresh and illuminating perspective on the surge in religion's political influence across the globe.[17] And despite recent claims that religion is exclusively irrational and violent, its political influence is in fact diverse, sometimes promoting civil war and terrorism but at other times fostering democracy, reconciliation, and peace. In our diverse and sort of 'mixed' world today, the forces of secularism are at work in our age of reason and science despite trends in fanaticism and inclinations of selected politicians attempting to use religion for political gains in several parts of the world. I contend that despite mixed messages on the subject, forces for secularism with its various components may play a sobering influence in keeping a handle on the forces of religious intolerance and extremism.

Terrorists and terrorist organizations, including governments in a few countries, have taken an increased interest during the past few decades in articulating religious reasoning to rationalize or justify violent means for achieving their political and economic goals.[18] However, no formal religion in the world actually may have condoned violence against innocent people. I stated earlier in Chapter 6 that the institution of religion has been misused by some people for political or whatever reasons. It seems that it is time we reverse the cycle and advocate its "right or proper" use in human relationships, i.e. for initiatives against violence. Contemporary societies need to develop and adopt an optimistic tone that seeks to find the future-oriented ways of preventing religion-based terrorism or any other related form of violence against the humanity and enhance the opportunities for the promotion of secularism and a global peace.

I take the position that secularism, as functioning process and practice in any society, needs to be acceptable to people just as much or even more than it is to their government. It is an ideology and a source of liberating human beings from dogma, superstitions, cultism, and any form of fanaticism. It emphasizes that people's attitudes toward other religions in their society need to become positive toward the freedom and equality in matters of conscience and freedom in exercising religion with a 'secular mind'.[19] Secularism demands religious groups give flexibility to people in civil matters. Thus, religion may need to maintain some degree of neutrality in dealing with individuals' private lives.

CHARACTERISTICS OF SECULARISM

I discussed in Chapter 1 the Delphi methodology that has been used in my research for developing typologies and characteristics of various notions presented in this book. I have in the exploratory study reported here at least made a beginning toward identifying selected ideal characteristics of secularism, first through a relatively extensive review of literature relevant to the topic and then by consulting some 'experts' in trying to sort as well as rank those characteristics in as much meaningful way as could be possible in a limited effort addressing a complex topic inherently plagued by confusions, philosophical controversies, and a lack of research that could solidify logical and empirical dilemmas.

The characteristics appear to be realistic, internally consistent, theoretically meaningful, and conceptually relevant to secularism. However, they should be repeatedly tested, through a systematic methodology, in empirical contexts for reliability and validity before becoming established in the literature. My identification of multiple characteristics organized under topics of multiple categories should be useful for continuous efforts needed in broadening the operational definition as well as the base of the concept of secularism. Indeed, matters of rationality and religion will require people to continue to engage in dialogs and open communication in order to deal with such sensitive issues as what we are dealing with in this chapter.

Separation of Religion and State

- Assure all people an equal liberty of conscience (or conviction/faith) in society. Constitutional principles and civil laws relevant to a secularist perspective in the state should be explicitly stated and implemented.

- No oppression of any religion should be permitted. State shall promote or recognize formally any dominant religion. Political candidates should refrain from publically advocating any particular religion in democratic elections.

- Implement a completely free exercise of religion, along with a prohibition of economic and political controls, regulation, or interference from government in affairs of all religions.

- Assure an unconditional judicial monitoring and protection to all ethnic and religious minorities from domination by majorities.

- Fully implement through all branches of the government (executive, legislative and judiciary), the accommodation principle, the non-establishment principle, and separation of each religion in the country and state.

- Guarantee the state's neutrality by avoiding the establishment of any particular religion and in basing civil and criminal jurisprudence on logical and democratic processes than on any scripture of faith.

- Provide people an unconditional and full confidence in the impartial and independent judiciary as well as a fair and effective law enforcement system without the use of any religious favoritism.

- Assure avoidance to people of any dependence on any religious control from any possible national or international sources, or from some specific person(s) of charisma or other form of authority.

- Encourage and implement a policy of non-alliance and neutrality in every religion in the country to pursue any political activities or parties by cultivating a desire among its believers for promoting and focusing only on pursuing spiritual activities.

Modernism and Religion

- Low degree of cultist and orthodox orientations in religions.

- Advocacy of moderate, tolerant, non-militant, open-minded, and humanist (rather than inflexible, rigid, fanatic, fundamentalist, authoritarian, heroworship-oriented, enthusiast, domineering; aggressive, expansionist, separatist, intrusive, or radical) outlook in every religion.

- There should be no public bashing of any religion.

- Separation of religion from educational programs (specifically, promote no schooling of children solely brainwashing them for any religious training) which must be based on academic freedom and scientific enquiry.
- Separation of religion from magical, fatalist, or superstitious approaches; every religion recognizing individualism, equality, and freedom for all people.
- Preventing all religious organizations from engaging in a business model or from soliciting monetary charges for 'divine favors or interventions' to help people overcoming life problems.
- Promote freedom to people to practice whatever level of religiosity they choose in terms of participation in religious rituals and organizations.
- Increased emphasis on spirituality as the primary goal of religion; and religious organizations recognizing needs and realities of change and rationality-oriented progress in society.
- Increased recognition for non-violence and humanitarian goals and outlooks in religion and spirituality.
- Secularism reinforces critical and diverse thinking; a process that promotes unity in diversity.

Pluralism in Religious Outlook and Practice

- Allow no law enforcement labeling or profiling based on religion.
- Make every possible effort for resolving conflicts among various religious groups through negotiations, collaboration, and civility.
- Promote religious diversity and a spirit of pluralism without recognizing any form of segregation and ranking of various religions.
- Inculcate a sense of and public's positive attitude toward co-existing, tolerating, and accepting people of different faith voluntarily without prejudice.

- Provide legal protection to people of all religions from any acts involving persecution, reprisals, threats, aggressiveness, intrusiveness, retaliation, harassment, or hate crimes.
- Provide reasonable accommodation to people of minority religions.
- Encourage mass media agencies to treat people of all religions with professionalism and objective reporting by not promoting or spreading fears or phobias about any religion.
- Promote non-obsessive/non-manipulative outlooks in every religious movement enhancing the scope of peace, non-violence and goodwill.

CONCLUDING REMARKS

The chapter identified several examples of the preventive strategies for terrorism, included a few characteristics of secularism. It is clear that secularism can play a significant role in affecting the terrorist movement in the contemporary world. Chapter 8 will further illustrate secularism as I try to envision non-violence as an ideal way to accomplish success in prevention.

8

Nonviolence for the Future of Mankind

But I say unto you, That ye resist not evil: but whosoever shall smite thee on thy right cheek, turn to him the other also.—Love your enemies and pray for those who persecute you.

—Matthew 5:39-44

My optimism rests on my belief in the infinite possibilities of the individual to develop nonviolence. The more you develop it in your being, the more infectious it becomes till it overwhelms your surroundings and by and by might oversweep the world.

—Mahatma Gandhi

To punish and destroy the oppressor is merely to initiate a new cycle of violence and oppression.

—Thomas Merton

Peace is more than the absence of war; it is a state of tranquility founded on the deep sense of security that arises from mutual understanding, tolerance of others' point of view, and respect for their rights.

—Dalai Lama

Nonviolence is the solution to conflict. I say the solution because there are no others. Because, if you return evil for evil, you are not putting an end to evil, you are doubling it.

—Lanza del Vasto

THE IDEOLOGY OF NONVIOLENCE

I talked about a defense of a conceptual perspective employing ideological and idealistic ideas for constructive purposes in Chapter 1. In Chapter 7, I examined selected ideological strategies, including secularism, relevant to preventing violence in general and terrorism in particular. As a concluding chapter in the book, I am now presenting selected ideas on nonviolence. It is possible that I indulge in this chapter in some 'wishful' and 'what is desirable' thinking occasionally using even 'utopian'[1] or 'mythical' notions or arguments. Examples of many so-termed ideologies have traditionally included "ideas defending a social position or promoting a program of social action".[2]

Nonviolence is an outlook for understanding and improving human relations. It does not necessarily imply a 'false consciousness'[3] of well-being. It seems that some degree of idealism, even utopianism, of nonviolence may be desirable and even a rational choice as compared to options such as the destruction of our future. Despite the challenges involved in materializing various pacifistic and nonviolent strategies, several leaders[4] in the past struggled in conceptualizing and advocating nonviolent ideologies.[5] It seems that those efforts have been, at least in some ways, instrumental in providing human beings alternative guidelines as options to indulging in serious forms of violence in relationships. Nonviolence perspective that was once considered to be too metaphysical and idealistic in the past seems to be one of the most effective ways of combating terrorist activities into the future.

Is non-violence merely an absence and/or elimination of violence, or is this concept adequately unique in its own independent meaning? After engaging in a serious reading of the relevant literature on the subject, I have concluded that the concept of nonviolence has its own identity, far more meaningful than merely doing away with violence. For example, nonviolence (without a hyphen in the middle) is not dialectical, contrary or opposite notion to that of violence. On the other hand, it represents an independent outlook with a connotation of highly suggestive meanings. Although human beings may not be able to eliminate violence from life (as it is a reality in nature as well as in society in some ways), we still need to develop ideas for effectively overcoming that violence as much as possible.

Several religious and other beliefs[6] have identified goals of nonviolence (such as peace, equality, secularism, and love),[7] and desirable means for achieving its goals (such as forgiveness, patience, not practicing neutrality to addressing violence, non-aggressive orientation, exclusion of a flight from the scene of violence, and no practice of capitulation or submission/surrender to anyone). Progress is visualized by some with signs of hope such as traditional war now is rather becoming obsolete and counter-productive in nuclear age. Instead, possibilities seem to be realized by people in some countries to bring change in their governments through some form of nonviolent revolutions. It seems to be possible to manage and correct man's destructiveness through rational and peaceful means. While nonviolent change may be slow, it is often more enduring than the change brought about by force. Peace can be far more enduring if conflicts and violent tendencies are resolved 'creatively' and continuously according to a number of peace and security studies conducted in Europe during the past few decades.[8] Despite of a rather non-scientific implication of the European peace studies, they addressed realities of social inequalities that have produced latent conflicts in the contemporary world. It is important that we recognize that a stable peace is possible through on-going conflict resolutions based on international socio-political justice, environmental security and human rights.

LOGICAL ASSUMPTIONS FOR ADVOCATING NONVIOLENCE

On the basis of my understanding of ideas relevant to nonviolence, I am stating below a few examples of assumptions for confirming nonviolent strategies to have potentials for making a difference in dealing with violence and terror in the world. These assumptions are based on a logic drawn from an extensive review of literature. However, assumptions are tentative ideas to get us started to think about possibilities of nonviolence and allow additional ideas and critical thinking develop in the future on them through counter-arguments and elaborations in the literature.

1. The assumption that human beings are a violent species has not been scientifically proven. On the other hand, humans are known for compassion, kindness, helping fellow beings in need, family values, loving interests, communication skills, and rational orientations.

2. There have been pieces of historical evidence of nonviolent strategies succeeding in achieving social and political justice in several parts of the world.

3. Some of the examples of personality orientations of nonviolent people are being identified as: calm, self-reliant, mature, autonomous, unprejudiced, open, selfless, civil, ethical, non-manipulative, believing in both equality and freedom, voluntaristic, and being tolerant of diversity.

4. Injustice is a state of violence. Refusing to obey injustice is just. Some people may have bowed heads before genociders such as Genghis Khan, Hitler, Mussolini, and Stalin who were perhaps 'defeated and power hungry' historical figures to begin with.

5. Historically, the institutionalized violence called 'war' seems to have been an 'easier' choice of those in power than options chosen for developing prospects for peace and nonviolence.

6. Nonviolence is based on ethical or moral grounds assuming that human beings in general have compassion and would do what is 'right' and not what is 'prudent' for achieving socialized goals.

7. Truth and justice generally prevail at lease in the long run.

8. Persuasion is more 'forceful' than physical coercion. Aggression involves a destructive component, hence it is always hazardous. Constructive energy provides individual greater inner confidence than muscular strength needed for violent aggression.

9. Curbing particular terrorist groups or destroying their leaders may not necessarily end the cycle of violence.

10. Escalation of conflicts can be reduced through rationally and democratically based negotiations. I am basically assuming that democratic processes are more congenial to nonviolence than those based on monarchies, aristocracies, dictatorships, theocracies, and so forth.

11. Nonviolent communications can be increased through mass media and educational programs. Nonviolent means can resolve conflicts through goodwill, winning hearts not conquering bodies. The pacifist approach has no emphasis on conquest and generally is more effective in achieving peace in the long run.

12. Nonviolent means are more 'curative' solutions than the 'band-aid' strategies through warfare. Nonviolence pursues humility without strife, gentleness, fearlessness, selflessness, and disarmament. Constant persistence with a determination for a just cause works more than extensive massacres and exterminations.

13. Nonviolence costs less than violent actions. Nonviolence does not entail defeat, humiliation, revenge or retaliation. Being humble is not cowardice.

14. Nonviolence believes in relationship building, partnership, communication, acceptance, and involvement.

15. Give and take negotiation relies on the exchange principles that are based on convincing the rival parties through reason possibly leading toward a process of adjustment and not dominance.

16. Nonviolence is based on the hope that our younger generations are increasingly alienated from wars, terror, and destruction. Therein may reside solutions based on lasting peace in the future.

17. Nonviolence pursues cool and composed approach not believing in quick fixes; it is a substantive outlook and not empty words.

NONVIOLENCE BASED ON THREE MAJOR PRINCIPLES

I have conceptualized three principles of nonviolence, along with goals and means for each as indicated in Table 8.1. The principles of (1) Assertiveness, (2) Democratic Values, and (3) Religious and Cultural Harmony are illustrated in that table and then discussed further in the chapter.

Table 8.1: Three Major Principles and Goals of Nonviolence along with Means for the Achievement of Each

Types of Nonviolence Principles	Goals of Each Principle	Means for Achieving Goals
I. **Assertiveness**	1. Courage	1. Passive Resistance and Non-Obedience to the Unjust Authority
	2. Authenticity (Being Genuine)	2. Pursue Truth and Justice; Overcome Hypocrisy
	3. Autonomy	3. Achieve and Maintain Self Regard and Independence
II. **Democratic Values**	1. Freedom and Voluntarism	1. End Foreign Occupations, Theocracies and Dictatorships
	2. Balance of Power in Three Branches of Government	2. Government. Based on People's Involvement and Consensus
	3. Equal Opportunity	3. Implement Rule of Law and Due Process
III. **Religious and Cultural Harmony**	1. Overcome Fear and Prejudice	1. Vitalize Selflessness or Altruism and Accomplish Secularism
	2. Achieve Multiculturalism and Pluralism	2. Promote Pluralistic Interactions and Dialogs
	3. Healing, Coexistence, Tolerance, Empathy. Trust, Peace and Hope	3. Negotiate and Resolve Conflicts

1. Nonviolence Based on Assertiveness

In my opinion, the major principle of nonviolence is assertiveness maintained in behaviors and attitudes by individuals and groups. The concept of assertiveness has been popularly used in social sciences, business, education, leadership training, and other fields. However, the usage of this notion seems to have often been rather simplistic neglecting its possible multiple indicators. My major goal is to explore a clarification of the concept of assertiveness in relation to nonviolence. I first developed a three-dimensional scale of assertiveness and then tested it for reliability and validity through the use of Delphi procedures described earlier in Chapter 1.

Assertiveness is an important concept in counseling, psychology, and sociology for dealing with issues in cross-cultural personality traits,[9] leadership development,[10] recovering mental health,[11] conflict management,[12] and overcoming discrimination and prejudice, including violence and exploitations involved in gender relationships.[13] However, the literature on assertiveness is loaded with a formula type of definition of this concept. For example, a large number of books and articles use 'how to become assertive' approach without any conceptual, theoretical, or methodological sophistication on the subject.[14]

I am probably the first sociologist who focused on the conceptualization and measurement of assertiveness as relevant to nonviolence. Parts of my methodology used here have been developed and empirically tested in previous studies involving measurements of constructs such as prevention of violence,[15] adjustment to single parenthood,[16] and commitment to marriage.[17] For the purposes of this study, assertiveness was treated as a process[18] and defined in a social-psychological sense, i.e. in terms of an individual's own perceptions or interpretations of how assertive he or she feels in his or her relationships.[19] I first identified a typology of three indicators of various styles of assertiveness in human relationships based on a thorough review of literature and theoretical relevance or logic.[20] Although additional or other related indicators of assertiveness are possible and likely to exist in the existing literature on the subject, I focused on three indicators only.

Details on assertiveness and its indicators are illustrated by Figure 8.1 further outlined in Table 8.2 and then briefly discussed.

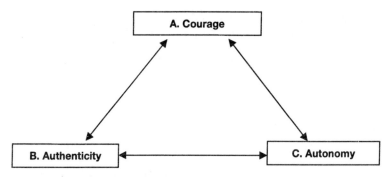

Fig. 8.1: Three Inter-related Indicators of Assertiveness

Table 8.2: Concepts or Characteristics of Behaviors or Attitudes under Each Indicator of Assertiveness

Courage	Authenticity	Autonomy
• self esteem	• says 'no' without guilt	• independent
• self regard	• self acceptance	• self-sufficient
• expresses feelings, opinions & preferences	• being oneself; attitude of imperfection	• makes own decisions
• takes responsibility of own actions	• legitimate	• self-confident
• leader	• truthful; honest	• open for change
• problem solver	• straight forward	• makes choices
• bold; daring	• direct	• accommodating
• gutsy	• expressive	• tolerant of diversity
• takes stand	• spontaneous	• flexible
• seeks justice & right; not being forced	• affective	• respects others' freedom & rights
• unafraid; fearless	• genuine	• reciprocates
• risk taker	• legitimate	• strong 'I'
• will not compromise central values	• frank; non-ambivalent	• maintains integrity
• plans & acts	• fair	• rational
• responds to criticism	• candid	• puts no limits on self
• imperfectionist	• modest	• happy
• non-authoritarian	• predictable	• adjusted
• non-domineering	• compassionate	• deals with issues
• has core values	• creative	• sociable

Courage

There is no shortage of literature on courage, given that humanity has been recording tales of courage since the invention of writing.[21] Courage is an important aspect of an assertive behavior or personality.[22] As indicated in Table 8.2, it is represented by characteristics such as strong self-confidence, self-regard, guts, boldness, fearlessness, non-submissiveness (but non-aggressiveness), straightforwardness, achievement striving, and leadership.[23] Courageous persons do not readily compromise their principles or convictions and have the ability to take risk without being concerned of the adverse consequences. They have strength of character, zest for life, perseverance, endurance, determination, and tend to feel that they are in control of their lives. They will confront even themselves when they feel they are wrong about making a decision. On the other hand, people who are no not courageous are likely to be aggressive, violent, dominant, authoritarian, egotistical, perfectionists, rash, hateful, demanding, blunt, arrogant, controlling, and even repressive.[24] Non-courageous people also tend to generally have behavioral characteristics such as being timid, passive, fearful, cowardice, selfish and distrustful, along with an inferiority complex. There is also a relationship between courage and voluntarism. People who are confident of themselves may not be led into doing things based on coercion and sense of obligation as such. They tend to choose things they want to do. Nonviolence implies a kind of bravery far different from violence.[25] For example, while being courageous one may sometime assume that any dialog with opposition will mean defeat. However, courage involves fortitude, strength to bear pain, and tolerance. It does not necessarily involve taking a fight or fleeing from the scene of conflict. Instead, a courageous person does not accept injustice from anyone and confronts the unjust person in defiance and is prepared to face consequences. Road to peace, justice and nonviolence is often not easy and restful and may involve a struggle.

Judges in this study ranked the characteristics of a nonviolent person with courage in the following manner:

1. Having self-confidence and self-regard

2. Is bold and active

3. Is unafraid and non-fearful

4. Is a risk taker in an unselfish cause

5. Takes responsibility of own actions

6. Is influential without seeking recognition and power

7. Is non-submissive and non-timid taking stand for what is right

8. Believes in pursuing what is right, including, for example, courage to oppose illegally or unethically torturing terrorist suspects and takes stand on issues and strategies that are not politically popular.

Authenticity

Authenticity, as one of the traits of assertiveness, involves the individual being honest, spontaneous or genuine (rather than being artificial or pretentious, or having a 'false front'), straight forward (being able to say 'no' without feeling guilty), frank, and candid (having candor in taking responsibility). It is based on a total awareness and understanding of one's self, plus an honest assessment and appraisal of one's personality.[26] Even though humans are not necessarily fully authentic, they reach different levels of authenticity through their life experiences.[27]

The concept of a 'just war' is quite meaningful in being relevant to the process of authenticity and implies "the great challenge of our time is how to achieve justice, with struggle, but without war".[28]

The notion of 'truth' is closely connected to authenticity. Belief in truth of course is too complex to be easily comprehended or defined. Examples of two aspects of truth are stated as follows.

(a) **Truth and Reality.** Truth is usually conceived as something valid, contrary to falsehood. The ontological level of truth refers to the 'absolute' reality which exists regardless of the extent of our knowledge of it. It is the objective reality based on 'universal' criteria. The phenomenological truth, on the other hand, is subjectively experienced or perceived reality as defined through the individual's interpretation. With this separation of the content of truth from the feeling of trueness, there is revealed to us the problem of truth and reality in its complete practical meaning, as well as in its psychological and epistemological aspect.[29] It is imperative that authentic behaviors such as involving nonviolent outlook through 'satyagraha'[30] (or house of truth and holding onto truth), are genuine in order to be effective in making a difference in the process of justice.

(b) **Sociocultural Meaning of Truth.** There is always consistency between authentic people's inner experiences and outer expressions of these inner experiences because of social and cultural expectations based on social norms or rules of behaviors. For example, inauthentic people are often found to be manipulative, conniving, inhibited or covert (rather than confronting reality), judgmental, and go around in life engaging in game playing with others and keeping a façade according to the demand of the social environment. Sociologists have recognized that there is an 'oversocialized' conception of man in society and asserted that inauthentic behaviors occur any time one gets engaged in dealing with the world by conforming to conventional ways of thinking and behaving.[31]

Judges in my study ranked the characteristics of authenticity in the following manner:

1. Being genuine and spontaneous
2. Being truthful, non-manipulative and honest
3. Being frank, straight forward and candid
4. Being open to criticism
5. Being loyal to one's true self, without pretense
6. Having to say no without feeling guilty
7. Being affective and compassionate (rather than being hateful and vindictive).

Autonomy

Autonomy (or freedom) is also an integral component of assertiveness. Autonomous people are generally independent (economically, socially, and emotionally), relatively self-sufficient, and are likely to make their own decisions. They tend to be flexible, change-oriented, open-minded, tolerant of diversity, and respectful of other people's freedom and rights. At the phenomenological level, human autonomy is reflected in the experience of integrity, volition, and vitality that accompanies self-regulated action.[32] It seems that the level of differentiation in a person is on a continuum. At one end is autonomy, which gives the ability to an individual to think through situation independently and clearly. And at the other end, there is a fusion whereby the individual is undifferentiating which results in emotional dependency on others. Without autonomy and internal locos of control, one cannot experience competence in assertiveness fully.[33] Proponents of the self-determination theory maintain that autonomy is an innate psychological need of human beings. Psychologists believe that autonomy is related to the experience of integration and freedom and plays a crucial part in healthy human functioning.[34] Researchers also associate self-esteem with behaving autonomously. Drawing from the 'self-determination theory' that looks at the individual's autonomy in a relationship as an innate need, some even claim that obstruction of satisfaction of this need will result in a low self-esteem. Nonviolence outlook does not go for defeat when someone has a 'just' cause. It is founded on the unshakable firmness and determination based on love not lust. It has a firm resistance to force while defending on the basis of truth and 'right' cause. It does not go for any 'vindictiveness' nor any passive surrender. The non-cooperation movement "is a protest against an unwitting participation in evil".[35]

Judges in this study ranked the characteristics of autonomy in the following manner:

1. Being determined to making own decisions
2. Having a sense of self-sufficiency and freedom
3. Avoids dependency and enslavement to others as well as material goods
4. Being tolerant of differences among others and is respectful of everyone's freedom

5. Being open for change

6. Having a sense of contentment (or adaptation and adjustment rather than being 'in a state of war' with anxiety and conflict) in the present state of life.

Inter-relationships among Indicators of Assertiveness

Courage, authenticity, and autonomy as indicators of the assertiveness process are assumed in this study as being conceptually and logically inter-related or inter-connected to one another. One cannot, for example, fully experience courage without being authentic and vice versa.[36] In the same way, one cannot actualize courage in real behaviors without having some sense of autonomy.[37] One needs to be courageous enough to take the risk and communicate one's intra experience regarding the relationship without fear of negative consequences. Moreover, authenticity cannot be achieved without autonomy as one's sense of independence leads to self-acceptance and self-regard. Overall, autonomy is the first step in having courage to be who one is or wants to be.

2. Nonviolence Based on Democratic Values

Rousseau made an assertion in one of his writings that "Man was born free but now is in chains." Man's freedom to him became less of a concern in the name of social order. However, as I indicated earlier in this chapter under the subtopic of autonomy, freedom and independence are important needs of human beings.

It has been demonstrated again and again in human history that a democratic system of government (as compared to monarchies, aristocracies, dictatorships, communist so-called 'classless' societies, theocracies, or whatever other system humans may have tried) has a 'better' potential for providing citizens opportunities for fundamental rights, rule of law, due process through an independent judicial system, popular sovereignty, and decentralization of power. This judgment is not mine alone; a large number of scholars in the civilized world have some degree of consensus on the above statement despite of comments such as possibilities of unequal opportunities for the exercise of freedom by all citizens.[38] Of course, there is probably no system devised by humans that may be 'perfect'. We just have to keep on protecting people's freedom by reforming democratic processes involved in legislating and executing laws.

A number of political scholars have expressed that democracies do not fight with each other.[39] The democratic countries seem to have generally have formed stable relations with each other and often organize international alliances based on economic and political interests and traditions such as advocating human rights and for stabilizing international law and order by controlling rogue dictators.

The governments of free societies, for example, charged with fighting a rising tide of terrorism, are thus faced with a democratic dilemma: If they do not fight terrorism with the means available to them, they endanger their citizenry; if they do, they appear to endanger the very freedoms which they are charged to protect. It is important to note that countries that engage in terrorist groups and/or sponsor terrorist activities have lately been theocracies or some form of dictatorship. However, some of them may formally have 'democratic systems' but may covertly support terrorism. These arguments seem to rest on the implicit assumption that foreign policy among democracies needs to be transparent and that decision makers in democratic states should have adequate information about what each is doing that might negatively affect each other's interests. That should help avoid possibilities of suspicion and misunderstanding about covert terrorist activities. A climate or spirit of nonviolence would, therefore, be less likely to overcome adversarial relations among nations and, subsequently, less likely to create international violence.[40]

Peace-making efforts of democracies in general seem to be becoming regular traditions in order to be effective. Their relatively liberal and open communication should continue to create trust and confidence into each other. Many of them have been engaged in improving quality of life as well as security of people. Some have worked on improving the world's security by 'fighting' selected sources of terror. They have been addressing terror democratically, even considering possibilities of negotiating with terrorists.[41]

Democracy is a difficult and complex term to define and apply in a nation under the shadow of war and terror. Terrorism is likely to be a threat to democratic peace.[42] For example, questions such as ones stated below have been raised in the media during the past few years as part of some critical thinking in order to demonstrate concerns about needs for protecting democratic identity during the period of engagement by various countries in the so-called 'war against terrorism'.

(1) To what degree a democratic nation continues to maintain principles of democracy when facing terrorist attacks? Are adequate laws enacted to protect and maintain those principles during crises caused by violent attacks?

(2) Are prisoners of war given access to the due process historically established at national and international levels?

Overall, one of the major democratic principles is to let people rule themselves and not be coerced into any form of government they may not want. Foreign occupations of nations, including any form of colonization, are most likely not in the spirit of democracy. Human history seems to have already demonstrated eventual failures of those who forcefully and arbitrarily occupy territories or countries.

Other principle so vital to a democracy consists of the 'freedom of press' and responsible journalism based on a significant level of communication and interconnectivity among people. In addition, each democratic country needs in principle to have an independent judiciary so people's rights are protected. A true democracy is significantly pluralistic, recognizing diversity as well as equality of opportunities for all people. We are living in a global and progressive age and need to broaden outlook of future generations through educational institutions that maintain academic freedom without any controls or interferences from religious and political influences on schools in civil society based on the public good.

The bottom lines for the success of democracies is for people *staying involved* and *actively engaged* in making sure that the spirit of democracy is meaningfully maintained and upheld. A democratic society promotes people's right to dissent, including 'passive resistance' and 'civil disobedience' in nonviolent ways. Pacifism is a commitment to peace and opposition to war. Pacific means peacemaking, involving a rejection of an overemphasis on militarism. However, pacifism is not passivism; it is active resistance and implies an opposition to war and commitment to nonviolence. People in a democracy have the right to engage in peaceful protests.

3. Nonviolence Based on Religious and Cultural Harmony

Independence of Each Religion

I devoted Chapters 6 and 8 to critically examine the role of religion in violence as well as the issue of equality and freedom of faith through the notion of secularism. The process of nonviolence requires that all religions and religious groups/organizations in the world become adjusted and accommodating to each other through mutual respect and coexistence. Religious and spiritual harmony among people would enhance the scope of tolerance and appreciation of each other's right to own convictions without labeling, stereotyping or judging each other for being different. As stated earlier in Chapter 6, most religious organizations have generally kept some degree of tolerance toward each other historically despite scattered incidents of violence (some quite serious) based on religion. However, an awareness of the need for adjusting to religious diversity should be continuously created all over the world in every possible way.

Persons as well as groups, small or large, need to avoid ranking different religions on the bases of whatever criteria, including the size of congregation and whether a religion is relatively older or newer. Each religious group needs to maintain neutrality and respectability toward other religious groups and organizations without any sense of relative deprivation or inferiority/superiority complex on the basis of any criteria whatsoever. Religious harmony will require tolerance of diversity of ideologies as well as of religious rituals at people's homes or places of worship. Any form of adversity or hate among religions should be avoided in every possible way. No attempts are needed for assimilating or integrating world religions by leaving people alone for making own choices for their personal and/or group's convictions. The age of mass conversions of people into any religion through force or persuasions seems to be over. There needs to be maximum civility[43] of interactions among people of diverse faith.

Recognizing Cultural Relativity and Diversity

The term 'cultural relativity' was introduced mainly by anthropologists for recognizing the uniqueness of each culture in defining truth and social norms for judging social behaviors for being 'right' or 'wrong'. Classical sociologists such as Durkheim also stressed that "social structures must be assessed not in relation to some absolute, ethnocentric, or moralistic standard but in their own terms and in view of the particular cultural context in which they are found".[44]

The importance of cultural relativity has increased in the world today. The globalization trends have enhanced the scope of interactions among nations and people at large. Those trends have obviously multiplied diversity in almost every country and region of the globe. Mass media as well as technological revolution have facilitated increased availability of knowledge and awareness of cultural differences among people. Ignorance of cultural differences among people is not considered to be bliss by business organizations as well as by governments engaged in international security issues. High rates of mobility as well as googled types of sources of information are likely to create avenues of a universality of mass culture.

However, I do not mean to imply that families, communities, and individuals are losing a sense of identity of own cultural uniqueness. It is likely that people increasingly cling to own cultural heritage in today's cosmopolitan world. Overall, trends of individualism are on the rise. Diverse cultures, therefore, are increasingly becoming divisive and diffused, needing an attention to the development of or improvements in moral values relevant to altruism and selflessness among people.

There is a growing concern about human beings consistently loosing humane and compassionate qualities due to a rising trend in materialism, selfishness, greed, and a lack of concern for the public good.[45] We need to reverse trends of self-centeredness and hedonism in the mankind and start recovering traditional moral outlook based on qualities such as tolerance, integrity and sacrifice for what is good for our future survival and prosperity. It is only by cultivating those qualities that we may be able to reverse the trends of serious forms of violence through rational negotiations for disarmament and peace on this planet.

CONCLUDING COMMENTS

My final chapter in the book demonstrates my optimism and emphasis on a constructive, though idealistic, outlook of examining the possibility of nonviolence and broadmindedness for dealing with the problem of terrorism. I outlined logical assumptions and principles of nonviolence, including examples of their indicators, goals, and means. I have in this chapter provided you only an overview of selected concepts and principles relevant to serious notions and hope that I got you interested in seeking additional information for grasping the depth of their meanings and implications for our future well-being.

Nonviolence types of ideals shall be implemented only if the world leaders realize that one of the ways to move toward such ideals can only be through a resolve that affirms that we stop occupying foreign territories even for short durations with noble intentions. A recent study, for example, provides meaningful data showing that foreign military occupation, or the imminent threat of it, is the root cause of terrorism. The stationing of foreign combat forces (ground and tactical air force units) on territory that terrorists prize accounts for 87 per cent of the over 1800 suicide terrorist attacks around the world since 2004.[46] It seems nonviolence may be a possible strategy for reducing terrorism around the globe if our leaders start working on strategies different from what some of them have been doing in the past. I hope nonviolence becomes an important notion in practice than one that only sits in a library shelf.

Endnotes

Chapter 1

1. Bellamy, 2008, p. 135.
2. Unnithan *et al.*, 1994, p. 2.
3. Whiteneck, 2008; Weber, 1949; McKinney, 1966.
4. The forthcoming reader on terrorism edited by Horgan and Braddock. 2012; Lutz and Lutz, 2008.
5. Barber, 1995. He developed the idea of a "McWorld," with greater opportunities for a global-capitalist-economy.
6. Paul and Elder, 2010: www.criticalthinking.org
7. Yinger (1965) elaborates on various levels of analysis based on the so-called "field theory of behavior."
8. Marx and Engels, 1930.
9. See, for example, Martindale, 1960; Hadden, 1997; Delaney, 2004.
10. See, for example, Barreto, 2005; Bellamy, 2008; Darwin, 1859; Farber, 1868; Green, 1979; Hoffer, 1951; Marx and Engles, 1930; Menninger, 1938; Mills, 1959; Nay, 2004.
11. See, for example, Durkheim, 1951; Pope, 1976.
12. See, for example, Delaney, 2004; Faure and Zartman, 2010; Frey, 2006; Martindale, 1960; Pape and Feldman, 2010.
13. Homans, 1950.
14. Weber, 1949.
15. See, for example, Kfir, 2002; Mead, 1934; Rank, 1964; Yinger, 1965.
16. Allport, 1955, advocated a need to analyze human personality in the process of "becoming" rather than a complete of finished entity.
17. Singh and Wilkinson, 1974; Yinger, 1965.

18. Historical and classificatory 'ideal' types are based on "reconstructions of past events, or ideas, in which some aspects are accentuated so that they are logically (or rationally, to use Weber's word) integrated and complete." Turner *et al.*, 1995, p. 196. I also followed the typology construction methodology spelled out by McKinney, 1966.

19. Singh and Webb, 1979.

20. Custer, Scarcella and Stewart, 1999.

Chapter 2

1. Audi, 1971, p. 50. Examples of violent behaviors are listed by the author on pp. 51-52.

2. Quoted in Tolan, 2007, p. 7.

3. Adorno *et al.*, 1950; Eller, 2006.

4. Gilligan, 1996, pp. 94-95.

5. Arendt, 1969, p. 79.

6. Eller, 2006, p. 8.

7. Tolan, 2007, p. 11.

8. Putney and Putney, 1964.

9. Adorno *et al.*, 1950; Canto-Sperber, 2006.

10. Darwin, 1859.

11. Martindale, 1960, pp. 144-47.

12. Darwin, 1880.

13. Scott, 1976, p. 21.

14. Straussner and Phillips, 2004.

15. Eller, 2006, pp. 34-35.

16. Scott, 1976, p. 15; Wilkinson, 1979, p. 46; Lorenz, 1966, p. 172.

17. Bumiller, 1990.

18. Eller, 2006, p. 38.

19. Lorenz, 1966.

20. Collins, 2008.

21. Freud, 1946.

22. Agnew, 2007.

Chapter 3

1. Pedahzur, 2005; Reuter, 2004.

2. Joshi *et al.*, 2002; Juergensmeyer, 2003; Selengut, 2003.

3. Homer-Dixon, 2008; Howard, 2008; Lutz and Lutz, 2004.

4. Weinberg *et al.*, 2012, p. 76.

5. Kapitan and Schulte, 2002, p. 172.

6. Howard and Hoffman, 2012.

7. See, for example, Weinberg, Pedahzur and Hirsch-Hoefler, 2012.

8. Crotty, 2005, pp. 5-10.

9. Hamden, 2002, p. 165.

10. *Ibid.*, 2002, p. 166.

11. Wilkinson, 1979, p. 45.

12. For example, the Geneva Convention spelled out the just cause of warfare.

13. Kapitan and Schulte, 2002, p. 181.

14. This is in reference to the *Mahabharata* war at Krukshetra in ancient India. See Ockrent, 2006, p. 89.

15. Sellmann, 2011, pp. 415-16.

16. Russell and Miller, 1979, pp. 8-10.

17. Swami, 2003 illustrating the case of Tamil Tigers.

18. Lutz and Lutz, 2011, p. 732.

19. Carr, 2002.

20. For example, bombings in Europe in World War II.

21. Sellmann, 2011, p. 416.

22. Dolan, 2002, pp. x-xi.

23. Lutz and Lutz, 2011, pp. 732-33.

24. Martin, 2010, pp. 220-65.

Chapter 4

1. Hoffer, 1951, pp. 1-3.

2. Lutz and Lutz, 2008, p. 3.

3. For example, in Kashmir, Iraq, Israel, Afghanistan, and Pakistan.

4. Menninger, 1938, pp. 16-18.

5. Maris, 1991; Kubler-Ross, 1969.

6. Pape and Feldman, 2010, pp. 3-9.

7. Joshi *et al.*, 2002; Juergensmeyer, 2003; Selengut, 2003.

8. Pape and Feldman, 2010, p. 5.

9. Kushner, 1998.

10. Durkheim, 1951.

11. Kfir, 2002.

12. Maris, 1991.

13. Menninger, 1938, p. 140 calls them as 'unmoral'.

14. Maris, 1991, pp. 361-62.

15. Plutchik, 2000, pp. 414-15.
16. Goldblatt and Silverman, 2000, pp. 140-41.
17. Collins, 2008, p. 446.
18. Bloom, 2006.
19. Durkheim, 1951.
20. Pape, 2005, p. 61.
21. Orum, 2001, p. 5.
22. For example, Al Quaidas used American financial and training resources, planes, and perhaps with a little own funding to cause one of the most deadly forms of destruction in the world history on September 11, 2001.
23. Perliger, 2011, p. 720.
24. *Ibid.*
25. Pape, 2005, p. 121.
26. In reference to the 9/11 event in 2001.
27. This is in reference to Tamil Tigers who have recently been very seriously impacted after their leaders' death in encounter in Sri Lanka.

Chapter 5

1. Stillion and McDowell, 1996.
2. Ardila, 2002.
3. Mack, 2002.
4. Grotberg, 2002.
5. Douglas, 1967; Goertzel, 2002; Collins, 2008.
6. Singh and Abbassi, 2005.
7. See, for example, Pescosolido and Georgianna, 1989.
8. Bellamy, 2008; Levin, 2007.
9. Klausen's 2005 analysis illustrating how the Islamic groups in Europe have been adopting a rather liberal outlook in order to adapt to a democratic political style.
10. Pape, 2005, p. 18. Faure and Zartman, 2010, p. 6, also note that "investigations have shown that there is no clear correlation between poverty and terrorism".
11. See implications of this theory for dealing with terrorism in Madhu, 2003; Netanyahu, 1995; Nicholson, 1961; and Pape, 2003.
12. Homans, 1950.
13. Lawal, 2002.

14. Examples of recent separatist movements include Palestinians, Tamil Tigers in Sri Lanka, Khalistan movement in north India, and so forth.

15. Hess and Kalb, 2003. In a note in the book, Steve Talbot, president of the Brookings Institution stated: "If indeed we are heading into an age in which we fully exercise the freedom technology gives us to be the editor-in-chief of the news we can consume, that will push us more in direction of atomized and perhaps in some cases antagonistic sub-communities, exacerbating our differences along cultural, partisan, and ideological lines."

16. The London subway bombing, the Intifadas, the Oslo shooting, and 9/11 are examples of this mindset.

17. Anderson, 1993.

18. Turvey, 1999.

19. Keskin-Kozat, 2006 for the 9/11 event.

20. Strausner, 2004, pp. 9-10.

21. Reuter, 2004.

22. Strausner, 2004, pp. 4-8. See additional literature on the victimization process.

23. Numerous articles and research findings were published, for example, after the 9/11 event in the U.S.

24. Simonsen and Spinlove, 2004, p. 3.

25. Keskin-Kozat, 2006.

Chapter 6

1. See four volumes on the subject edited by Ellens, 2003.

2. Sharot, 2001; Weber, 1964.

3. Selengut, 2003, p. 1.

4. Selengut, 2003, p. 3. The author talks on pp. 9-10 about 'religious violence to include (1) physical injury or death, (2) self-mortification and religious suicide, (3) psychological injury, and (4) symbolic violence causing the desecration or profanation of sacred sites and holy places.

5. Demerath III and Hammond, 1969.

6. Feldman, 2006; Dolan, 2002.

7. Critchley, 2008, p. xv.

8. Sharot, 2001.

9. Erikson, E., 1958.

10. Allport, G.W., 1955; Hadaway and Roof, 1978.

11. See, for example, Hoffer, E., 1951; and Homans, G., 1950.
12. Turner, 1980.
13. Kubler-Ross, 1969, stages of death and dying, including denial, anger, bargaining, depression and acceptance.
14. See, for example, Sen, 2007.
15. Vivekananda, 1946.
16. Weber, 1964, as one of the prominent sources for establishing the contribution of religion to development of social norms.
17. Marx and Engels, 1930.
18. Weber, 1950.
19. See, for example, Weber, 1964; Toft, Philpot and Shah, 2011; Taubmann, 2006.
20. Hill and Hood, 1999.
21. Adorno, Brunswik, Levinson and Sanford, 1950; Amon, 1982; Anderson, 2011; Barreto, 2005; Bloom, 2006; Carr, 2002; Demerath III and Hammond, 1969; Farrell, A.D. and Vulin-Reynolds, 2007; Gilligan, 2006; Goertzel, 2002; Hafez, 2006; Hrynkow, 2011; Juergensmeyer, 2003; Laqueur, 1999; Lutz and Lutz, 2011; Piszkiewicz, 2003.
22. Phillips, 2006.

Chapter 7

1. Russell, 1962.
2. Sartre and Levy, 1996; Forni, 2002.
3. Homer-Dixon, 2008; Howard, 2008; Lutz and Lutz, 2004.
4. Bellamy, 2008, p. 135.
5. Unnithan *et al.*, 1994, p. 2.
6. Whiteneck, 2008.
7. Alexander, 2006.
8. Toft *et al.*, 2011.
9. Ardila, 2002.
10. Pape and Feldman, 2010.
11. Perliger, 2011.
12. Pape, 2005.
13. Piszkiewicz, 2003.
14. Reid, 2002.
15. Reuter, 2004.
16. Selengut, 2003.
17. Sen, 2007.

18. Shank and Erwin, 2011.
19. King, 2007, pp. 9-44.

Chapter 8

1. Karl Mannheim, 1936.
2. Martindale, 1960, p. 127.
3. Marx and Engles, 1930, argued that a "false consciousness" of well-being by the proletarians leads to their exploitation by the bourgeoisies.
4. See, for example, religious leaders such as Jesus Christ and Gautama Buddha, and political figures such as Mahatma Gandhi and Martin Luther King. In his 2006 book on *Global Problems: The Search for Equity, Peace, and Sustainability,* Sernau outlines a history of "moral leadership as resilience" provided by several figures on nonviolent exemplary themes making significant contributions in that regard in various parts of the globe.
5. Gandhi, 1957; Huxley, 1937; Muste, 1940; Steinkraus, 1973; Unnithan and Singh, 1973.
6. Unnithan and Singh's illustrations of advocacy of nonviolence in the Judaic and Christian traditions, Islamic faith, Hinduism, and Chinese traditions; and see Ross, 2011, for example, of other sources of belief in nonviolence such as Baha'ism, Jainism, Pacifism, Sufism, Unitarian Universalism, and Zen Buddhism.
7. Russell, 1962; Galtung, 1996.
8. Some of the ideas on the subject are expressed in Random edited del Vasto, 1974, p. 4; Sernau, 2006, pp. 222-23; Schell, 2003; and Charney, 1982, pp. 50-57. For peace and security studies, see Galtung, 1996; Lawler, 2008.
9. Cooley and Nowicki, 1984; Hofstede, 1998; Costa, Terracciano and McCrae, 2001; Twenge, 2001; Farver, Narang and Bhadha, 2002; Rahman and Rao, 2004.
10. Bower and Bower, 1991.
11. Jakubowski and Lange, 1978; Enns, 1992; Braiker, 2001.
12. Bishop, 1997.
13. Bloom, Coburn and Perlman, 1975; Phelps and Austin, 1975; Butler, 1981; Gallois and Wilson, 1993; Goodman and Fallon, 1998; Alberti and Emmons, 2001; Neff and Harter, 2002; Rudrappa, 2004.
14. See, for example, Adama and McNeilage, 1982; Baer, 1976; Cotler and Guerra, 1976; Lloyd, 1988; Lindenfield, 1992; Paterson, 2000; Burns, 2001.
15. Singh and Abbassi, 2008.

16. Singh and McBroom, 1992.
17. Singh and Kanjirathinkal, 1999.
18. See Allport, 1955.
19. Mead, 1934.
20. Weber, 1949.
21. Miller, 2000, p. x.
22. Tillich, 1952.
23. See, for example, Costa *et al.*, 2001; Twenge, 2001; Buss, 2004.
24. See, for example, Moran, 1956; Kateb, 2004.
25. Merton, 1965, p. 13.
26. Neff and Harter, 2003.
27. Smith, 1991.
28. Zin, 2004.
29. Rank, 1936, p. 40.
30. Gandhi (1957:75) asserted: "It is better to be violent, if there is violence in our hearts, than to put on the cloak of nonviolence to cover impotence."
31. Wrong, 1961, pp. 183-84.
32. Cooley and Nowicki, 1984; Beyers, Vansat and Moore, 2003.
33. See, for example, Deci and Ryan, 2000.
34. Braiker, 2001.
35. Merton, 1965.
36. Twenge, 2001.
37. Costa *et al.*, 2001.
38. Mills, 1956, demonstrated, for example, how a minority of citizens in the U.S. enjoy greater opportunities for power and freedom than most citizens. Marx had made that clear through his criticism of capitalism.
39. For example, the NATO operations recently in Libya.
40. Schell, 2003.
41. Sellmann, 2011; Faure and Zartman, 2010.
42. Barreto, 2005; Sen, 2007.
43. Forni, 2002.
44. Durkheim, 1951, p. 71.
45. Lasley, II, 1994, pp. 3-8.
46. Pape, 2005.

References

Abdullah, S. (2002). "The Soul of a Terrorist: Reflections on Our War with the 'Other'", pp. 1-8 in C.E. Stout ed. *The Psychology of Terrorism: A Public Understanding.* Vol. I. Westport, Conn.: Praeger.

Adama, K.A. and McNeilage, L.A. (1982). *Assertiveness at Work: How to Increase Your Personal Power on the Job.* Englewood Cliffs, NJ: Prentice-Hall.

Adorno, T., et al. (1950). *The Authoritarian Personality.* New York: Harper.

Agnew, R.S. (2007). "Strain Theory and Violent Behavior", pp. 519-29 in D.J. Flannely, A.T. Vazsonyi and I.D. Waldman ed. *The Cambridge Handbook of Violent Behavior and Aggression.* New York: Cambridge University Press.

Alberti, R. and Emmons, M. (2001). *Your Perfect Right: Assertiveness and Equality in Your Life and Relationship.* New York: Impact Publishers.

Alexander, Y. (2006). "Responses to Terrorism: Some Political and Legal Perspectives", pp. 181-88 in D.S. Hamilton ed. *Terrorism and International Relations.* Washington, DC: Center for Transatlantic Relations.

———. (1979). "Terrorism and the Media", pp. 159-74 in Y. Alexander, D. Carlton and P. Wilkinson ed. *Terrorism: Theory and Practice.* Boulder, CO: Westview Press.

Allport, G.W. (1955). *Becoming: Basic Considerations for Psychology of Personality.* New Haven, CT: Yale University Press.

Amon, M. (1982). "Unraveling of the Myth of Progress", pp. 62-76 in D.C. Rapoport and Y. Alexander ed. *The Morality of Terrorism: Religious and Secular Justifications.* New York: Pergamon Press.

Anderson, T. (1993). "Terrorism and Censorship: The Media Chains", *Journal of International Affairs*, 47: 127-36.

Anderson, O. (2011). "Philosophical Perspectives", pp. 557-66 in J.I. Ross ed. *Religion and Violence: An Encyclopedia of Faith and Conflict from Antiquity to the Present*, Vol. 2. New York: M.E. Sharpe.

Arendt, H. (1969). *On Violence.* New York: Harcourt, Brace, and the World.

Ardila, R. (2002). "The Psychology of the Terrorist: Behavioral Perspectives", pp. 9-16 in C.E. Stout ed. *The Psychology of Terrorism: A Public Understanding*, Vol. I. Westport, Conn.: Praeger.

Asad, T. (2007). *On Suicide Bombing.* New York: Columbia University Press.

Atkinson, J.M. (1978). *Discovering Suicide: Studies in the Social Organization of Sudden Death.* Pittsburgh, PA: University of Pittsburgh Press.

Audi, R. (1971). "On the Meaning and Justification of Violence", pp. 45-100 in J.A. Shaffer ed. *Violence: Award Winning Essays in the Council for Philosophical Studies Competition.* New York: David McKay.

Baer, J. (1976). *How to be Assertive (Non Aggressive) Woman in Life, in Love, and on the Job.* Bergenfield, NJ: Penguin.

Bajpai, K.P. (2002). *Roots of Terrorism.* New York: Penguin.

Balkin, K. (Ed.) (2005). *Poverty: Opposing Viewpoints.* Farmington Hills, MI: Greenhaven Press.

Barber, B. (1995). *Jihad vs. McWorld.* New York: Times Books.

Barreto, A.A. (2005). "Toward a Theoretical Explanation of Political Extremism", pp. 17-31 in W. Crotty ed. *Democratic Development and Political Terrorism: The Global Perspective*. Boston, MA: Northwestern University Press.

Beck, A.T., Schuyler, D. and Herman, I. (1986). "Development of Suicidal Intent Scales", pp. 45-58 in A.T. Beck, H.L.P. Resnik and D.J. Lettieri ed. *The Prediction of Suicide*. Philadelphia, PA: The Charles Press.

Bellamy, A.J. (2008). "Conflict Prevention and the Responsibility to Protect", *Global Governance* 14, 135-56.

Benjamin, D. (2006). "Religion and Civilization", pp. 63-72 in D.S. Hamilton ed. *Terrorism and International Relations*. Washington, DC: Center for Transatlantic Relations.

Beyers, W., et al. (2003). "A Structural Model of Autonomy in Middle and Late Adolescence: Connectedness, Separation, Detachment, and Agency." *Journal of Youth and Adolescence*, 32, 351-65.

Bhargava, R. (2007). "What is Secularism For?" pp. 486-542 in R. Bhargava ed. *Secularism and Its Critics*. New Delhi: Oxford University Press.

Bilgrami, A. (2007). "Secularism, Nationalism, and Modernity", pp. 380-417 in R. Bhargava ed. *Secularism and Its Critics*. New Delhi: Oxford University Press.

Bishop, S. (1997). *Training Game for Assertiveness and Conflict Resolution*. New York: McGraw-Hill.

Bloom, M. (2006). "Dying to Kill: Motivations for Suicide Terrorism", pp. 25-53 in A. Pedahzur ed. *Root Causes of Suicide Terrorism: The Globalization of Martyrdom*. New York: Routledge.

Bloom, L.Z., Coburn, K. and Perlman, J. (1975). *The Assertive Woman*. New York: Delacorte.

Borgeson, K. and Valeri, R. (2009). *Terrorism in America*. Boston, MA: Jones and Bartlett.

Bower, S.A. and Bower, G.H. (1991). *Asserting Yourself: Practical Guide for Positive Change.* Reading, Mass.: Addison-Wesley.

Braiker, H.B. (2001). *The Disease to Please: Curing the People-Pleasing Syndrome.* New York: McGraw-Hill.

Browne, Harry. (2001). Preventing Future Terrorism. Online Available: http://antiwar.com.html. November 1.

Bruce, S. (2002). *God is Dead: Secularization in the West.* Malden, MA: Blakwell.

Bumiller, E. (1990). *May You be the Mother of a Hundred Sons: A Journey Among the Women of India?* New York: Fawcett Columbine.

Burns, R. (2001). *Making Assertiveness Happen: A Simple and Effective Guide to Developing Assertiveness Skills.* Waniewood, Australia: Business Publishing.

Buss, A.H. (2004). "Anger, Frustration, and Aversiveness", *Emotion,* 4, 131-32.

Butler, P. (1981). *Self Assertion for Women.* San Francisco, CA: Harper and Row.

Canto-Sperber, M. (2006). "Terrorism and Just War", pp. 103-14 in D.S. Hamilton ed. *Terrorism and International Relations.* Washington, DC: Center for Transatlantic Relations.

Carr, C. (2002). *The Lessons of Terror.* New York: Random House.

Castle, T. (2011). "Self Immolation", pp. 669-73 in J.I. Ross ed. *Religion and Violence: An Encyclopedia of Faith and Conflict from Antiquity to the Present.* Vol. 3. New York: M.E. Sharpe.

Charny, I.W. (1982). *How Can We Commit the Unthinkable? Genocide: The Human Cancer.* Boulder, CO: Westview Press.

Chatterjee, P. (2007). "Secularism and Tolerance", pp. 345-79 in R. Bhargava ed. *Secularism and Its Critics.* New Delhi: Oxford University Press.

Cigler, A.J. (Ed.) (2002). *Perspectives on Terrorism: How 9/11 Changed U.S. Politics*. Boston: Houghton Mifflin.

Collins, R. (2008). *Violence: A Micro-Sociological Theory*. Princeton, NJ: Princeton University Press.

Cooley, E.L. and Nowicki, S. (1984). "Locus of Control and Assertiveness in Male and Female College Students", *The Journal of Psychology*, 117, 85-87.

Cooley, J.K. (2000). *Unholy Wars: Afghanistan, America and International Terrorism*. London: Pluto Press.

Cortright, D. (2008). *Peace: A History of Movements and Ideas*. Cambridge: Cambridge University Press.

Costa, P.T., Terracciano, A. and McCrae, R.R. (2001). "Gender Differences in Personality Across Cultures: Robust and Surprising Findings", *Journal of Personality and Social Psychology*, 81, 322-31.

Crelinsten, R.C., Leberge-Almejd, D. and Szabo, D. (1978). *Terrorism and Criminal Justice: An International Perspective*. Lexington, MA: Lexington Books.

Critchley, S. (2008). *The Book of Dead Philosophers*. New York: Vintage Books.

Crotty, W. (2005). "Democratization and Political Terrorism", pp. 3-16 in W. Crotty ed. *Democratic Development & Political Terrorism: The Global Perspective*. Boston, MA: Northwestern University Press.

Custer, R.L., Scarcella, J.A. and Stewart, B.R. (1999). "The Modified Delphi Technique: A Rotational Modification." *Journal of Vocational and Technical Education*, 15: 63-72.

Dahlberg, L.L. (2007). "Public Health and Violence: Moving Forward in a Global Context", pp. 465-485 in J. Flannery, A.T. Vazsonyi and I.D. Waldman ed. *The Cambridge Handbook of Violent Behavior and Aggression*. New York: Cambridge University Press.

Darwin, C. (1859). *On the Origin of Species by Means of Natural Selection*. London: J. Murray.

———. (1880). *The Descent of Man*. New York: D. Appleton.

Davies, T. and O'Keefe, B. (1987). "The Members of the International Task Force on Prevention of Nuclear Terrorism", pp. 7-50 in P. Leventhal and Y. Alexander ed. *Preventing Nuclear Terrorism*. Lexington, MA: D.C. Heath.

Davis, M. (2007). *Buda's Wagon: A Brief History of the Car Bomb*. London: Verso.

Davis, J.M. (2002). "Countering International Terrorism: Perspectives from International Psychology", pp. 33-56 in C.E. Stout ed. *The Psychology of Terrorism: Programs and Practices in Response and Prevention*. Vol. IV. Westport, Conn.: Praeger.

Delaney, T. (2004). *Classical Social Theory: Investigation and Application*. Upper Saddle River, NJ: Pearson/Prentice Hall.

Demerath III, N.J. and Hammond, P.E. (1969). *Religion in Social Context: Tradition and Transition*. New York: Random House.

Diggory, J.C. (1986). "Predicting Suicide: Will-o-the-Wisp or Reasonable Challenge?" pp. 59-70 in A.T. Beck, H.L.P. Resnik, and D.J. Lettieri ed. *The Prediction of Suicide*. Philadelphia, PA: The Charles Press.

Dobson, C. and Payne, R. (1982). *Counterattack: The West's Battle Against the Terrorists*. New York: Facts on File, Inc.

Dolan, C. (2002). *Religion on Trial*. Long Beach, CA: Mopah Publications.

Douglas, J.D. (1967). *The Social Meaning of Suicide*. Princeton, NJ: Princeton University Press.

Dublin, L.I. (1963). *Suicide: A Sociological and Statistical Study*. New York: The Ronald Press.

Dugard, J. (1982). "International Terrorism and the Just War", pp. 62-76 in D.C. Rapoport and Y. Alexander ed. *The Morality of Terrorism: Religious and Secular Justifications*. New York: Pergamon Press.

Durkheim, E. (1951). *Suicide: A Study in Sociology*. New York: The Free Press.

Egendorf, L.K. (Ed.) (2000). *Terrorism: Opposing Viewpoints*. San Diego: Greenhaven.

Egger, S.A. (2002). *The Killers Among Us*. Upper Saddle River: Prentice Hall.

Eikmeier, D.C. (2008). "Qutbism: An ideology of Islamic-Fascism", pp. 126-33 in T.J. Badey ed. *Violence and Terrorism*. New York: McGraw Hill.

Ellens, J.H. (Ed.) (2003). *The Destructive Power of Religion: Violence in Judaism, Christianity, and Islam*. Volumes 1-4. Westport, CT: Praeger.

Eller, J.D. (2006). *Violence and Culture: A Cross-Cultural and Interdisciplinary Approach*. Belmont, CA: Wadsworth.

Elliott, T.L. (2002). "Children and Trauma: An Overview of Reactions, Mediating Factors, and Practical Interventions That Can Be Implemented", pp. 1-26 in C.E. Stout ed. *The Psychology of Terrorism: Clinical Aspects and Responses*. Vol. II. Westport, Conn.: Praeger.

Emmott, B. (2008). *Rivals: How the Power Struggle Between China, India and Japan will Shape Our Next Decade*. New York: Harcourt.

Enns, C.Z. (1992). "Self-Esteem Groups: A Synthesis of Consciousness-raising and Assertiveness Training", *Journal of Counseling and Development*, 71, 7-13.

Erikson, E. (1958). *Young Man Luther*. New York: W.W. Norton.

Evans, G. (2006). "Responding to Terrorism", pp. 63-72 in D.S. Hamilton ed. *Terrorism and International Relations*. Washington, DC: Center for Transatlantic Relations.

Fabick, S.D. (2002). "Us and Them: Reducing the Risk of Terrorism", pp. 225-42 in C.E. Stout ed. *The Psychology of Terrorism: Clinical Aspects and Responses*. Vol. II. Westport, Conn.: Praeger.

Farber, M.L. (1968). *Theory of Suicide*. New York: Funk and Wagnalls.

Farberow, N.L. (Ed.) (1975). *Suicide in Different Cultures.* Baltimore, MD: University Park Press.

Farrell, A.D. and Vulin-Reynolds, M. (2007). "Violent Behavior and the Science of Prevention", pp. 767-86 in D.J. Flannely, A.T. Vazsonyi and I.D. Waldman ed. *The Cambridge Handbook of Violent Behavior and Aggression.* New York: Cambridge University Press.

Farrington, D.P. (2007). "Origins of Violent Behavior Over the Life Span", pp. 19-43 in D.J. Flannely, A.T. Vazsonyi and I.D. Waldman ed. *The Cambridge Handbook of Violent Behavior and Aggression.* New York: Cambridge University Press.

Farver, J.M., Narang, S.K. and Bhadha, B.R. (2002). "East Meets West: Ethnic Identity, Acculturation and Conflict in Asian Indian Families", *Journal of Family Psychology,* 16, 338-50.

Faure, G.O. and Zartman, I.W. (2010). *Negotiating with Terrorists: Strategy, Tactics and Politics.* New York: Routledge.

Fein, M. (1993). *I.A.M.: A Common Sense Guide to Coping with Anger.* Westport, Conn.: Praeger.

Feldman, N. (2006). *Divided by God.* New York: Farrar, Straus and Goroux.

Fields, R.M., Elbedour and Hein. (2002). "The Palestinian Bomber", pp. 193-224 in C.E. Stout ed. *The Psychology of Terrorism: Clinical Aspects and Responses.* Vol. II. Westport, Conn.: Praeger.

Flannery, D.J., Vazsonyi, A.T. and Waldman, I.D. (Eds.) (2007). *The Cambridge Handbook of Violent Behavior and Aggression.* New York: Cambridge University Press.

Forni, P.M. (2002). *Choosing Civility.* New York: St. Martin's Griffin.

Freud, S. (1946). *Civilization and Its Discontent.* London: Hogarth.

Frey, B.S. (2006). "Costs and Benefits of Anti-Terrorism Policies", pp. 169-81 in D.S. Hamilton ed. *Terrorism and*

International Relations. Washington, DC: Center for Transatlantic Relations.

Friedlander, R.A. (1979). "Coping with Terrorism: What Is To Be Done?" pp. 231-46 in Y. Alexander, D. Carlton and P. Wilkinson ed. *Terrorism: Theory and Practice.* Boulder, CO: Westview Press.

Galanter, M. (2007). "Hinduism, Secularism, and the Indian Judiciary", pp. 268-96 in R. Bhargava ed. *Secularism and Its Critics.* New Delhi: Oxford University Press.

Gallois, C. and Wilson, K. (1993). *Assertion and Its Social Context.* Terrytown: Pergmon Press.

Gandhi, M.K. (1957). *An Autobiography: The Story of My Experiments with Truth.* Boston: Beacon.

Galtung, J. (1996). *Peace by Peaceful Means: Peace, Conflict, Development and Civilization.* London: Sage and PRIO.

Gerstein, R. (1982). "Do Terrorists Have Rights?" pp. 290-307 in D.C. Rapoport and Y. Alexander ed. *The Morality of Terrorism: Religious and Secular Justifications.* New York: Pergamon Press.

Gil, F. (2006). "Conclusion", pp. 221-24 in D.S. Hamilton ed. *Terrorism and International Relations.* Washington, DC: Center for Transatlantic Relations.

Gilligan, J. (1996). *Violence: Reflections on a National Epidemic.* New York: Vintage Books.

Glasner, P.E. (1977). *The Sociology of Secularization: A Critique of a Concept.* London: Routledge and Kegan Paul.

Goertzel, T.G. (2002). "Terrorist Beliefs and Terrorist Lives", pp. 97-112 in C.E. Stout ed. *The Psychology of Terrorism: A Public Understanding.* Vol. I. Westport, Conn.: Praeger.

Goldblatt, M.J. and Silverman, M.M. (2000). "Physical Illness and Suicide", pp. 140-56 in Maris, R.W., Canetto, S.S., McIntosh, J.L. and Silverman, M.M. ed. *Review of Suicidology, 2000.* New York: The Guilford Press.

Goodman, M.S. and Fallon, B.C. (1998). *Pattern Changing for Abused Women*. Thousand Oaks, CA: Sage.

Green, L.C. (1979). "The Legalization of Terrorism", pp. 175-200 in Y. Alexander, D. Carlton and P. Wilkinson ed. *Terrorism: Theory and Practice*. Boulder, CO: Westview Press.

Grollman, E. (1988). *Suicide: Prevention, Intervention, Postvention*. Boston, MA: Beacon Press.

Grotberg, E.H. (2002). "From Terror to Triumph: The Path to Resilience", pp. 1-8 in C.E. Stout ed. *The Psychology of Terrorism: A Public Understanding*. Vol. I. Westport, Conn.: Praeger.

Hadaway, C.K. and Roof, W.C. (1978). "Religious Commitment and Quality of Life in America", *Review of Religious Research*, 19, 295-307.

Hadden, R.W. (1997). *Sociological Theory*. Peterborough, Ontario: Broadway Press.

Hafez, M.M. (2006). "Dying to be Martyrs: The Symbolic Dimension of Suicide Terrorism", pp. 55-80 in A. Pedahzur ed. *Root Causes of Suicide Terrorism: The Globalization of Martyrdom*. New York: Routledge.

Hamden, R.H. (2002). "The Retributional Terrorist: Type 4", pp. 165-92 in C.E. Stout ed. *The Psychology of Terrorism: Clinical Aspects and Responses*. Vol. II Westport, Conn.: Praeger.

Hamilton, D.S. (Ed.) (2006). *Terrorism and International Relations*. Washington, D.C.: Center for Transatlantic Relations.

Hanle, D.J. (1989). *Terrorism: The Newest Face of Warfare*. New York: Pergamon-Brassey.

Henderson, E.A. (2002). *Democracy and War: The End of an Illusion?* London: Lynne Rienner.

Herrick, J. (1985). *Against the Faith: Essays on Deists, Skeptics, and Atheists*. New York: Prometheus.

Hess, S. and Kalb, M. (Eds.) (2003). *The Media and the War on Terrorism*. Washington, D.C.: Brookings Institution Press.

Hill, P.C. and Hood, R.W. (1999). *Measures of Religiosity*. Birmingham, AL: Religious Education Press.

Hoffer, E. (1951). *The True Believer*. New York: Harper and Brothers.

Hofstede, G. (1998). *Masculinity and Femininity: The Taboo Dimensions of National Cultures*. Thousand Oaks, CA: Sage.

Homans, G. (1950). *The Human Group*. New York: Hartcourt and Brace.

Homer-Dixon, T. (2008). "Rise of Complex Terrorism", pp. 33-42 in R.D. Howard and J.J. Forest ed. *Weapons of Mass Destruction and Terrorism*. New York: McGraw-Hill.

Horgan, J. and Braddock, K. (Eds.) (2012). *Terrorism Studies: A Reader*. New York: Routledge.

Howard, R.D. and Hoffman, B. (Eds.) (2012). *Terrorism and Counterterrorism: Understanding the New Security Environment*. New York: McGraw-Hill.

Howard, R.D. (2008). "The New Terrorism and Weapons of Mass Destruction", pp. 6-22 in R.D. Howard and J.J. Forest ed. *Weapons of Mass Destruction and Terrorism*. New York: McGraw-Hill.

Hrynkow, C. (2011). "Conscientious Objection", pp. 206-12 in J.I. Ross ed. *Religion and Violence: An Encyclopedia of Faith and Conflict from Antiquity to the Present*. Vol. 1. New York: M.E. Sharpe.

Huxley, A. (1937). *An Encyclopedia of Pacifism*. New York: Harper and Bros.

Ivie, R.L. (2005). *Democracy and America's War on Terror*. Tuscaloosa: The University of Alabama Press.

Jakubowski, P. and Lange, A.J. (1978). *The Assertiveness Option*. Champaign, IL: Research Press.

Jenkins, B.M. (2006). *Unconquerable Nation: Knowing Our Enemy, Strengthening Ourselves.* Santa Monica: Rand Corporation.

Jenkins, P. (2003). *Images of Terror:* New York: Aldine de Gruyter.

Joshi, S., Walhof, D.R. and Peterson, D.R. (2002). *The Invention of Religion: Rethinking Belief in Politics and History.* New Brunswick, N.J.: Rutgers University Press.

Jucha, R. (Ed.) (2009). *Terrorism: An Interdisciplinary Perspective.* Belmont, CA: Wadsworth.

Juergensmeyer, M. (2003). *Terror in the Mind of God: The Global Rise of Religious Violence.* Berkeley: University of California Press.

———. (2006). "Debunking the Myths of Religious Terrorism", pp. 53-62 in D.S. Hamilton ed. *Terrorism and International Relations.* Washington, DC: Center for Transatlantic Relations.

Kaarthikeyan, D.R. and Radhavinod, R. (2004). *Rajiv Gandhi Assassination: The Investigation.* Chicago: New Dawn Press.

Kapitan, T. and Schulte, E. (2002). "The Rhetoric of 'Terrorism and Its consequences", *Journal of Political and Military Sociology,* 30 (1): 172-96.

Kateb, G. (2004). "Courage as a Virtue", *Social Research,* 71, 39-72.

Kerbo, H.R. (2003). *Social Stratification and Inequality.* New York: McGraw Hill.

Keskin-Kozart, B. (2006). "Grappling with 9/11 and its Aftermath: Reflections on the Collective Past, Present and Future Contemporary Societies", *International Sociology,* 21 (6): 815-21.

Kfir, N. (2002). "Understanding Suicide Terror Through Humanistic and Existential Psychology", pp. 143-58 in C.E. Stout ed. *The Psychology of Terrorism: A Public Understanding.* Vol. I. Westport, Conn.: Praeger.

Kilcullen, D. (2010). *Counterinsurgency.* New York: Oxford University Press.

King, M. (2007). *Secularism: The Hidden Origins of Disbelief.* Cambridge: James Clarke and Co.

Klausen, J. (2005). *The Islamic Challenge: Politics and Religion in Western Europe.* New York: Oxford University Press.

Kubler-Ross, E. (1969). *On Death and Dying.* New York: Routledge.

Kupperman, R. and Trent, D. (1999). *Terrorism: Threat, Reality, Response.* Stanford: Hoover Institution Press.

Kushner, H.W. (1998). *The Future of Terrorism: Violence in the New Millennium.* Thousand Oaks: Sage.

Lahey, B.B. (2007). "Personality Dispositions and the Development of Violence and conduct Problems", pp. 260-81 in D.J. Flannely, A.T. Vazsonyi and I.D. Waldman ed. *The Cambridge Handbook of Violent Behavior and Aggression.* New York: Cambridge University Press.

Laqueur, W. (1999). *The New Terrorism: Fanaticism and the Arms of Mass Destruction.* New York: Oxford University Press.

Lasley II, T.J. (1994). *Teaching Peace: Toward Cultural Selflessness.* Westport, Conn.: Bergin and Garvey.

Lawal, O.A. (2002). "Social-Psychological Considerations in the Emergence and Growth of Terrorism", pp. 23-32 in C.E. Stout ed. *The Psychology of Terrorism: Programs and Practices in Response and Prevention.* Vol. IV. Westport, Conn.: Praeger.

Lawler, P. (2008). "Peace Studies", pp. 88 in P.D. Williams ed. *Security Studies: An Introduction.* New York: Routledge.

Leach, M.M. (2006). *Cultural Diversity and Suicide.* New York: The Hayworth Press.

LeCapitaine, J.E. (2002). "Terror, Disaster, and War: How Can We Help Our Children?" pp. 183-94 in C.E. Stout ed. *The Psychology of Terrorism: Programs and Practices in Response and Prevention.* Vol. IV. Westport, Conn.: Praeger.

Levin, J. (2007). *The Violence of Hate: Confronting Racism, Anti-Semitism, and Other Forms of Bigotry.* New York: Pearson.

Lewis, O. (1959). *Five Families: Mexican Case Studies in the Culture of Poverty.* New York: Basic Books.

Litman, R.E. (1967). "Sigmund Freud on Suicide", pp. 132-57 in E. Shneidman ed. *Essays in Self Destruction.* New York: Science House.

Lloyd, S.R. (1988). *Developing Positive Assertiveness.* Menlo Park, Cal.: Crisp.

Lorenz, K. (1966). *On Aggression.* New York: Harcourt, Brace and World.

Lutz, B.J. and Lutz, J.M. (2011). "Terrorism", pp. 732-44 in J.I. Ross ed. *Religion and Violence: An Encyclopedia of Faith and Conflict from Antiquity to the Present.* Vol. 2. New York: M.E. Sharpe.

Lutz, J.M. and Lutz, B.J. (2008). *Global Terrorism.* New York: Rutledge.

Mack, J.E. (2002). "Looking Beyond Terrorism: Transcending the Mind of Enmity", pp. 173-84 in C.E. Stout ed. *The Psychology of Terrorism: A Public Understanding.* Vol. I. Westport, Conn.: Praeger.

Madhu, K.P. (2003). *Preventing Wars and Terrorism.* New Delhi: Mehta.

Mallampalli, C. (2004). *Christians and Public Life in Colonial South India, 1863-1937: Contending with Marginality.* New York: Taylor and Francis.

Maltsberger, J.T. and Buie, D.J. (1980). "The Devices of Suicide: Revenge, Riddance, and Rebirth", *International Review of Psychoanalysis*, 7: 61-72.

Marchisio, S. (2006). "Recent Developments in Anti-Terrorism Law: How to Fill Normative Gaps", pp. 113-46 in D.S. Hamilton ed. *Terrorism and International Relations.* Washington, DC: Center for Transatlantic Relations.

Marcus, E. (1996). *Why Suicide?* New York: Harper Collins.

Maris, R.W. (1991). *Pathways to Suicide: A Survey of Self-Destructive Behaviors.* Baltimore, MD: The John Hopkins Press.

Maris, R.W., Berman, A.L. and Silverman, M. (2000). *Comprehensive Textbook of Suicidology.* New York: The Guilford Press.

Martin, G. (2010). *Understanding Terrorism: Challenges, Perspectives, and Issues.* Los Angeles, CA: Sage.

———. (2008). *Essentials of Terrorism: Concepts and Controversies.* Thousand Oaks: Sage.

Martindale, D. (1960). *The Nature and Types of Sociological Theory.* Boston: Houghton Mifflin.

Marx, K. and Engels, F. (1930). *The Communist Manifesto.* New York: International Publishers.

Mayer, J.D. (2003). *9-11: The Giant Awakens.* Belmont, CA: Wadsworth.

McCarthy, S. (2002). "Preventing Future Terrorist Activities Among Adolescents Through Global Psychology: A Cooperative Learning Community", pp. 131-56 in C.E. Stout ed. *The Psychology of Terrorism: Programs and Practices in Response and Prevention.* Vol. IV. Westport, Conn.: Praeger.

McKinney, J.C. (1966). *Constructive Typology and Social Theory.* New York: Appleton-Century-Crafts.

Menninger, K.A. (1938). *Man Against Himself.* New York: Harcourt, Brace and Co.

Mead, G.H. (1934). *Mind, Self and Society.* Chicago: University of Chicago Press.

Merton, T. (1965). *Gandhi on Non-Violence.* New York: New Directions Publication.

Miller, W.I. (2000). *The Mystery of Courage.* Cambridge, Mass.: Harvard University Press.

Mills, C. Wright (1959). *The Sociological Imagination.* New York: Oxford University Press.

———. (1956). *The Power Elite*. New York: Oxford University Press.

Moran, L. (1956). *The Anatomy of Courage*. London: Constable.

Motto, J.A. (1986). "Refinement of Variables in Assessing Suicide Risk", pp. 85-93 in A.T. Beck, H.L.P. Resnik and D.J. Lettieri ed. *The Prediction of Suicide*. Philadelphia, PA: The Charles Press.

Moffat, G.K. (2006). *Violent Heart: Understanding Aggressive Individuals*. London: Praeger.

Moghadam, A. (2006). "Defining Terrorism", pp. 13-24 in A. Pedahzur ed. *Root Causes of Suicide Terrorism: The Globalization of Martyrdom*. New York: Routledge.

———. (2006). "The Roots of Suicide Terrorism", pp. 81-107 in A. Pedahzur ed. *Root Causes of Suicide Terrorism: The Globalization of Martyrdom*. New York: Routledge.

Muste, A.J. (1940). *Non-Violence in an Aggressive World*. New York: Harper and Bros.

Nacos, B.L. (2006). "Terrorism and Media in the Age of Global Communication", pp. 81-102 in D.S. Hamilton ed. *Terrorism and International Relations*. Washington, DC: Center for Transatlantic Relations.

Nandy, A. (2007). "The Politics of Secularism and the Recovery of Toleration", pp. 321-44 in R. Bhargava ed. *Secularism and Its Critics*. New Delhi: Oxford University Press.

Nay, W.R. (2004). *Taking Charge of Anger: How to Resolve Conflict, Sustain Relationships, and Express Yourself Without Losing Control*. New York: The Guilford Press.

Neff, K.D. and Harter, S. (2002). "The Authenticity of Conflict Resolution among Adult Couples?" *Sex Roles*, 47, 403-17.

———. (2003). "The Role of Power and Authenticity in Relationship Styles Emphasizing Autonomy,

Connectedness, or Mutuality among Adult Couples", *Journal of Social and Personal Relationships,* 19, 835-57.

Nellis, A. (2009). "Fear of Terrorism", pp. 117-47 in K. Borgeson and R. Valerie ed. *Terrorism in America.* Boston, MA: Jones and Bartlett.

Netanyahu, B. (1995). *Fighting Terrorism: How Democracies Can Defeat Domestic and International Terrorists.* New York: Harper Collins.

Nicolson, H. (1961). *The Age of Reason: The Eighteenth Century.* Garden City, NY: Doubleday.

Nussbaum, M.C. (2008). *Liberty of Conscience: In Defense of America's Tradition of Religious Equality.* New York: Basic Books.

Ockrent, C. (2006). "Media and Terrorism", pp. 73-80 in D.S. Hamilton ed. *Terrorism and International Relations.* Washington, DC: Center for Transatlantic Relations.

O'Connor, T.R. (2009). "The Criminology of Terrorism: Theories and Models", pp. 17-45 in K. Borgeson and R. Valerie ed. *Terrorism in America.* Boston, MA: Jones and Bartlett.

Orum, A.M. (2001). *Introduction to Political Sociology.* Upper Saddle River, NJ: Prentice Hall.

Pape, R.A. and Feldman, J.K. (2010). *Cutting the Fuse: The Explosion of Global Suicide Terrorism and How to Stop It.* Chicago: The University of Chicago Press.

Pape, R.A. (2005). *Dying to Win.* New York: Random House.

Parry, J.P. (1985). "Sources of Moral Judgement", pp. 200-25 in J. Overing ed. *Reason and Morality.* London: Travistock.

Paterson, R.J. (2000). *The Assertiveness Workbook: How to Express Your Ideas and Stand Up for Yourself at Work and in Relationships.* Oakland, CA: New Harbinger.

Paul, R. and Elder, L. (2010). *Critical Thinking: Concepts and Tools.* www.criticalthinking.org

Pedahzur, A. and Perliger, A. (2006). "Introduction: Characteristics of Suicide Attacks", pp. 1-12 in A.

Pedahzur ed. *Root Causes of Suicide Terrorism: The Globalization of Martyrdom.* New York: Routledge.

Pedahzur, A. (2005). *Suicide Terrorism.* Cambridge, U.K.: Polity Press.

Perliger, A. (2011). "Suicide Bombing", pp. 718-24 in J.I. Ross ed. *Religion and Violence: An Encyclopedia of Faith and Conflict from Antiquity to the Present.* Vol. 3. New York: M.E. Sharpe.

Phelps, S. and Austin, N. (1975). *The Assertive Woman.* San Luis Obispo, CA: Impact.

Phillips, K. (2006). *American Theocracy: The Peril and Politics of Radical Religion, Oil, and Borrowed Money in the 21st Century.* New York: Penguin Books.

Pilisuk, M. and Bosch, A. (2002). "State Terrorism: When the Perpetrator is a Government", pp. 105-32 in C.E. Stout ed. *The Psychology of Terrorism: Clinical Aspects and Responses.* Vol. II. Westport, Conn.: Praeger.

Piszkiewicz, D. (2003). *Terrorism's War with America: A History.* London: Praeger.

Plutchik, R. (2000). "Aggression, Violence, and Suicide", pp. 407-23 in Maris, R.W., Berman, A.L. and Silverman, M. ed. *Comprehensive Textbook of Suicidology.* New York: The Guilford Press.

Pokorni, A.D. (1986). "A Scheme for Classifying Suicidal Behaviors", pp. 29-44 in A.T. Beck, H.L.P. Resnik and D.J. Lettieri ed. *The Prediction of Suicide.* Philadelphia, PA: The Charles Press.

Pope, W. (1976). *Durkheim's Suicide: A Classic Analyzed.* Chicago, IL: The University of Chicago Press.

Putney, S. and Putney, G.J. (1964). *Normal Neurosis.* New York: Harper and Row.

Quester, G.H. (1982). "Eliminating the Terrorist Opportunity", pp. 325-56 in D.C. Rapoport and Y. Alexander ed. *The Morality of Terrorism: Religious and Secular Justifications.* New York: Pergamon Press.

Random, M. (Ed.) (1974). *Warriors of Peace: Writings on the Technique of Nonviolence by Lanza del Vasto*. New York: Alfred A. Knopf.

Rank, O. (1964). *Truth and Reality*. New York: W.W. Norton.

Redlick, A.S. (1979). "The Transnational Flow of Information as a Cause of Terrorism", pp. 73-98 in Y. Alexander, D. Carlton and P. Wilkinson ed. *Terrorism: Theory and Practice*. Boulder, CO: Westview Press.

Reeve, S. (1999). *The New Jackals: Ramzi Yousef, Osama bin Laden and the Future of Terrorism*. Boston: Northeastern University Press.

Reid, W.H. (2002). "Controlling Political Terrorism: Practicality, Not Psychology", pp. 1-8 in C.E. Stout ed. *The Psychology of Terrorism: A Public Understanding*. Vol. I, Westport, Conn.: Praeger.

Reuter, C. (2004). *My Life is a Weapon*. Princeton, NJ: Princeton University Press.

Ronczkowski, M.R. (2007). *Terrorism and Organized Hate Crime: Intelligence Gathering, Analysis, and Interrogations*. New York: CRC Press.

Ross, I.R. (Ed.) (2011). *Religion and Violence: An Encyclopedia of Faith and Conflict from Antiquity to the Present*. Vol. 1, 2, 3. New York: M.E. Sharpe.

Rudd, M.D. (2000). "Integrating Science into the Practice of Suicidology", pp. 47-83 in R.W. Maris, S.S. Canetto and M.M. Silverman ed. *Review of Suicidology, 2000*. New York: The Guilford Press.

Russell, B. (1962). *Has Man a Future?* New York: Simon and Schuster.

Russell, C.A., Banker, Jr., L.J. and Miller, B.H. (1979). "Out-Inventing the Terrorist", pp. 3-44 in Y. Alexander, D. Carlton and P. Wilkinson ed. *Terrorism: Theory and Practice*. Boulder, CO: Westview Press.

Sartre, J.P. and Levy, B. (1996). *Hope and Now: The 1980 Interviews*. Chicago: The University of Chicago Press.

Scarpa, A. and Raine, A. (2007). "Biological Bases of Violence", pp. 151-69 in D.J. Flannely, A.T. Vazsonyi and I.D. Waldman ed. *The Cambridge Handbook of Violent Behavior and Aggression*. New York: Cambridge University Press.

Schell, J. (2003). *The Unconquerable World: Power, Nonviolence, and the Will of the People*. New York: Holt.

Scott, J.P. (1976). "The Control of Violence: Haman and Nonhuman Societies Compared", pp. 13-34 in A.G. Neil ed. *Violence in Animal and Human Societies*. Chicago, IL: Nelson Hall.

Selengut, C. (2003). *Sacred Fury: Understanding Religious Violence*. New York: Altimira.

Sellmann, J.D. (2011). "Just War Theory", pp. 414-17 in J.I. Ross ed. *Religion and Violence: An Encyclopedia of Faith and Conflict from Antiquity to the Present*. Vol. 2. New York: M.E. Sharpe.

Sen, A. (2007). "Secularism and Its Discontents", pp. 454-85 in R. Bhargava ed., *Secularism and Its Critics*. New Delhi: Oxford University Press.

Sernau, S. (2006). *Global Problems: The Search for Equity, Peace and Sustainability*. Boston, MA: Pearson.

Sexton-Radek, K. (2002). "How Conflict Resolution Programming in Our Schools Addresses Terrorism Issues", pp. 157-82 in C.E. Stout ed. *The Psychology of Terrorism: Programs and Practices in Response and Prevention*. Vol. IV. Westport, Conn.: Praeger.

Shank, M. and Erwin, C. (2011). "Victims", pp. 775-87 in J.I. Ross ed. *Religion and Violence: An Encyclopedia of Faith and Conflict from Antiquity to the Present*. Vol. 3. New York: M.E. Sharpe.

Sharot, S. (2001). *A Comparative Sociology of World Religions: Virtuosos, Priests, and Popular Religion*. New York: New York University Press.

Shneidman, E.S. (2001). *Comprehending Suicide: Landmarks in 20th Century Suicidology.* Washington, DC: American Psychological Association.

———. (1971). "The National Suicide Prevention", pp. 19-32 in J. Zusman and D.L. Davidson ed. *Organizing the Community to Prevent Suicide.* Springfield, Ill.: Charles C. Thomas.

———. (1981). *Suicide Thoughts and Reflections, 1960-1980.* New York: Human Sciences Press.

Sibney, D. (2006). "The Terrorist Setting", pp. 11-16 in D.S. Hamilton ed. *Terrorism and International Relations.* Washington, DC: Center for Transatlantic Relations.

Simonsen, C.E. and Spindlove, J.R. (2004). *Terrorism Today: The Past, the Players, the Future.* Upper Saddle River, NJ: Prentice Hall.

Sinclair, A. (2003). *An Anatomy of Terror: A History of Terrorism.* London: Macmillan.

Singh, R.N. and Wilkinson, K.P. (1974). "On the Measurement of Environmental Impacts of Public Projects from a Sociological Perspective", *Water Resources Bulletin*, 55: 121-37.

Singh, R.N. and Webb, B.R. (1979). "Use of Delphi Methodology to Assess Goals and Social Impacts of a Watershed Project", *Water Resources Bulletin* 15: 136-41.

Singh, R.N. and McBroom, J.R. (1992). "On Measuring the Adjustment of Separated and Divorced Mothers to Parenting: A Proposed Scale", *Journal of Divorce and Remarriage*, 18, 127.

Singh, R.N. and Kanjirathinkal, M. (1999). "Levels and Styles of Commitment in Marriage: The Case of Asian Indian Immigrants", pp. 307-22 in J.M. Adams and W.H. Jones eds. *Handbook of Interpersonal Commitment and Relationship Stability.* New York: Kluwer/Plenum.

Singh, R.N. and Abbassi, A. (2008). "Preventing Suicide Terrorism: Opportunities and Challenges", pp. 3-14 in

Singh, M. and Singh, D.P. ed. *Violence: Impact and Intervention.* New Delhi: Atlantic.

Sivan, E. (1985). *Radical Islam, Medieval Theology and Modern Politics.* New Haven: Yale University Press.

Small, S.M. and Opler, M.K. (1971). "Suicide: Epidemiological and Sociologic Considerations", pp. 9-18 in J. Zusman and D.L. Davidson eds. *Organizing the Community to Prevent Suicide.* Springfield, Ill.: Charles C. Thomas.

Smith, D.E. (2007). "India as a Secular State", pp. 177-233 in R. Bhargava ed. *Secularism and Its Critics.* New Delhi: Oxford University Press.

Smith, Q. (1991). "Wilshire's Theory of Authentic Self", *Human Studies,* 14, 339-57.

Staub, E. (2002). "Preventing Terrorism: Raising 'Inclusively' Caring Children in a Complex World of Twenty-First Century", pp. 119-30 in C.E. Stout ed. *The Psychology of Terrorism: Programs and Practices in Response and Prevention.* Vol. IV. Westport, Conn.: Praeger.

Steinkraus, W.E. (1973). "Martin Luther King's Personalism and Non-Violence", *Journal of History of Ideas,* 34: 97-111.

Stillion, J.M. and McDowell, E.A. (1996). *Suicide Across the Life Span.* Washington, D.C.: Taylor and Francis.

Stokes, T. (2002). "Terror and Violence Perpetrated by Children", pp. 77-90 in C.E. Stout ed. *The Psychology of Terrorism: Programs and Practices in Response and Prevention.* Vol. IV. Westport, Conn.: Praeger.

Stout, C.E. (Ed. of 4 Vols.) (2002). *The Psychology of Terrorism: A Public Understanding.* London: Praeger.

Straussner, S.L.A. and Phillips, N.K. (2004). *Understanding Mass Violence: A Social Work Perspective.* Boston, MA: Pearson.

Swami, N.M.R. (2003). *Inside an Elusive Mind: Prabhakaran.* Delhi: Konark.

Tambiah, S.J. (2007). "The Crisis of Secularism in India", pp. 418-53 in R. Bhargava ed. *Secularism and Its Critics*. New Delhi: Oxford University Press.

Taubmann, F. (2006). "God: Dangerous Word, Necessary Word", pp. 47-52 in D.S. Hamilton ed. *Terrorism and International Relations*. Washington, DC: Center for Transatlantic Relations.

Taylor, C. (2007). "Modes of Secularism", pp. 31-53 in R. Bhargava ed. *Secularism and Its Critics*. New Delhi: Oxford University Press.

Tillich, P. (1952). *The Courage to Be*. New Haven, CT: Yale University Press.

Toft, M.D., Philpot, D. and Shah, T.S. (2011). *Gods Century: Resurgent Religion and Global Politics*. New York: W.W. Norton.

Tolan, P.H. (2007). "Understanding Violence", pp. 5-18 in D.J. Flannely, A.T. Vazsonyi and I.D. Waldman ed. *The Cambridge Handbook of Violent Behavior and Aggression*. New York: Cambridge University Press.

Turner, B.S. (1980). "The Body and Religion" in *The American Review of Social Sciences of Religion*, 4: 247-86.

Turner, J.H., Beeghley, L. and Powers, C.H. (1995). *The Emergence of Sociological Theory*. New York: Wadsworth.

Turvey, B. (1999). *Criminal Profiling: An Introduction to Behavioral Evidence Analysis*. San Diego, CA: Academic Press.

Twenge, J.M. (2001). "Changes in Women's Assertiveness", *Journal of Personality and Social Psychology*, 81, 133-45.

Unnithan, T.K.N. and Singh, Y. (1973). *Traditions of Non-Violence*. New Delhi: Arnold-Heinemann.

Vivakananda, S. (1946). *India and Her Problems*. Calcutta: Advita Ashrama.

Wallerstein, I. (1974). *The Modern World-System*. New York: Academic Press.

Warneka, T.H. (2002). "The Long Shadow of Our Hidden Dragon Shared Factors of Terrorism and Juvenile Violence", in C.E. Stout ed., *The Psychology of Terrorism: Programs and Practices in Response ·and Prevention*. Vol. IV. Westport, Conn.: Praeger.

Weber, M. (1949). "Objectivity in Social Science and Social Policy", pp. 50-112 in E.A. Shills and H.A. Finch ed., *The Methodology of the Social Science*. New York: Free Press.

Weber, M. (1950). *The Protestant Ethic and the Spirit of Capitalism* (Tr. by Talcott Parsons). New York: Scribners.

Weber, M. (1964). *The Sociology of Religion*. Boston: Beacon Press.

Weinberg, L., Pedahzur, A. and Hirsch-Hoefler, S. (2012). "The Challenges of Conceptualizing Terrorism", pp. 76-85 in Horgan, J. and Braddock, K. ed. *Terrorism Studies: A Reader*. New York: Routledge.

Weinberg, L. (2006). "Suicide Terrorism for Secular Causes", pp. 108-21 in A. Pedahzur ed. *Root Causes of Suicide Terrorism: The Globalization of Martyrdom*. New York: Routledge.

Wessells, M. (2002). "Terrorism, Social Injustice, and Peace Building", pp. 57-76 in C.E. Stout ed. *The Psychology of Terrorism: Programs and Practices in Response and Prevention*. Vol. IV. Westport, Conn.: Praeger.

White, J.R. (2004). *Defending the Homeland: Domestic Intelligence, Law Enforcement, and Security*. Belmont, CA: Wadsworth.

Whiteneck, D. (2008). "Deterring Terrorists: Thoughts on a Framework", pp. 336-45 in D.H. Russell and Forest, J.J. ed. *Weapons of Mass Destruction and Terrorism*. New York: McGraw-Hill.

Whittaker, D.J. (2004). *Terrorists and Terrorism in the Contemporary World*. New York: Routledge.

Wilkinson, P. (1982). "The Laws of War and Terrorism", pp. 308-24 in D.C. Rapoport and Y. Alexander ed.

The Morality of Terrorism: Religious and Secular Justifications. New York: Pergamon Press.

———. (1979). "Social Scientific Theory of Civil Violence", pp. 45-72 in Y. Alexander, D. Carlton and P. Wilkinson ed. *Terrorism: Theory and Practice.* Boulder, CO: Westview Press.

———. (1979). "Terrorist Movements", pp. 3-44 in Y. Alexander, D. Carlton and P. Wilkinson ed. *Terrorism: Theory and Practice.* Boulder, CO: Westview Press.

Winkler, C.K. (2006). *In the Name of Terrorism: Presidents on Political Violence in the Post-World War Era.* New York: SUNY Press.

Wrong, D. (1961). "The Oversocialized Conception of Man in Modern Sociology. *American Sociological Review,* 26, 183-93.

Yinger, J.M. (1965). *Toward a Field Theory of Behavior: Personality and Social Structure.* New York: McGraw-Hill.

Zakaria, F. (2003). *The Future of freedom: Liberal Democracy at Home and Abroad.* New York: Norton.

Zubin, J. (1986). "Observations on Nosological Issues in the Classical of Suicidal Behaviors", pp. 3-28 in A.T. Beck, H.L.P. Resnik and D.J. Lettieri ed. *The Prediction of Suicide.* Philadelphia, PA: The Charles Press.

Subject Index

bride burning, vii

collectivistic terrorcide, 39
    pseudo collectivistic, 39-40
    fanatical collectivistic, 40
conceptual thinking, 5
conflict perspective, 6
constructive reasoning, 5-6
critical thinking, 3-6
cyber attacks, vii

Delphi technique, 9-12
dominance, characteristics of, 15

family violence, vii
    scenarios of child abuse, 17

globalization, 3

honor killing, vii
hostility, characteristics of, 15

idealistic perspective, 7
interpersonal violence, vi
irrationality, characteristics of, 15-16

nonviolence, ix

logical assumptions for, 81-84
meaning and ideology of, 80-81
principles of, 84-96
    assertiveness, 84-91
      authenticity and truth, 84, 86, 88-89
      autonomy, 84, 86, 89-91
      courage, 84, 86-88
      inter-relationships among the above, 91
      means for achieving goals, 84
    democratic values, 91-94
      means for achieving goals, 84
    religious and cultural harmony, 94-96
      cultural relativity/ diversity, 95-96
      independence of religion, 94-95
      means for achieving goals, 84

objective outlook, viii

partition of India and Pakistan, v